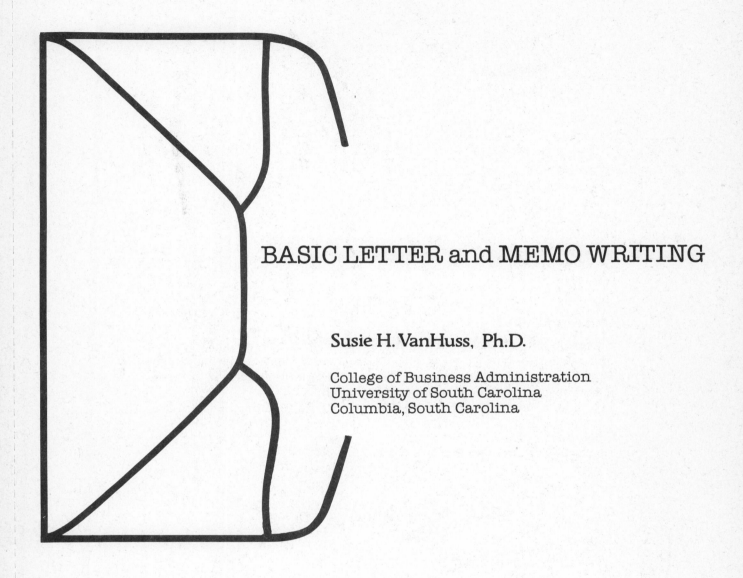

BASIC LETTER and MEMO WRITING

Susie H. VanHuss, Ph.D.

College of Business Administration
University of South Carolina
Columbia, South Carolina

E70

Published by

SOUTH-WESTERN PUBLISHING CO.

CINCINNATI   WEST CHICAGO, ILL.   DALLAS   PELHAM MANOR, N.Y.   PALO ALTO, CALIF.

ISBN: 0-538-05700-9
Library of Congress Catalog Card Number: 80-50473

4 5 H 5
Printed in the United States of America

PREFACE

BASIC LETTER AND MEMO WRITING is an intensive, activity oriented textbook-workbook designed to teach basic principles of writing and approaches for writing various types of communications. The text presents simplified guides and depends heavily on illustrations and exercises to teach basic writing principles.

Organization

This text is designed so that it can be used as (1) a basic text in letter and memo writing; (2) a supplemental text in a variety of courses such as Business English, English, Office Procedures, Cooperative Office Education, or other business and vocational courses; and (3) a self-teaching tool for anyone wanting to improve writing skills.

Illustrations presented are typical of communications written by entry-level employees in many different occupational clusters. Numerous exercises are used to apply the basic guides presented and illustrated.

Overview of Content

BASIC LETTER AND MEMO WRITING contains six chapters and an appendix. Each chapter consists of explanatory materials, illustrations, application exercises, and a performance evaluation. Two of the guides presented in Chapter 1 are reviewed in each of the following chapters. The appendix consists of illustrations of style and format for various types of communications.

Chapter 1, "Ten Easy Guides to Better Letters and Memos," analyzes and illustrates basic writing principles. Emphasis is placed on improving writing style.

Chapters 2, 3, and 4 present approaches for writing positive, neutral, and negative messages. For each type of message, an approach or model for writing is presented, explained, illustrated, and analyzed. Students are then given an opportunity to plan and write communications involving a variety of problem situations.

Chapter 5, "Writing Interoffice Memos," shows students how to adapt the basic models for positive, neutral, and negative letters to the writing of memorandums. The writing of short, informal reports in memorandum style is also introduced in this chapter with emphasis on organizational approaches and appropriate report writing style.

Chapter 6, "Job Application Communications," analyzes a variety of communications used in the employment process, including application letters, resumes, application forms, requests for recommendations, and letters of recommendation. This chapter gives an overview of the employment process from the perspective of both the employer and the individual seeking employment.

Appreciation

Appreciation is expressed to the following teachers and their students for field testing selected sections of the materials: Mrs. Andie Denton (Business English), Floyd D. Johnson Area Vocational Center, York, South Carolina; Mrs. Hoyland Fisher (Co-operative Office Education), Garrett High School, Charleston, South Carolina; Ms. Ann Jolly (Senior Intensified Program—Block), Daniel Morgan Area Vocational Center, Spartanburg, South Carolina; Mrs. Miriam Fisher (Office Practice), Dreher High School, Columbia, South Carolina.

The excellent suggestions presented by these teachers helped to make the materials more realistic and relevant.

Susie H. VanHuss

CONTENTS

Chapter 1   Ten Easy Guides to Better Letters and Memos   1

             Guide 1   Plan Before Writing   1

             Guide 2   Use the *You* Approach   5

             Guide 3   Use a Positive Approach   8

             Guide 4   Check for Accuracy   10

             Guide 5   Make Your Letters Simple and Easy to Understand   13

             Guide 6   Make Sure Your Letters Are Complete   19

             Guide 7   Use Specific, Concrete Language   21

             Guide 8   Use Words Efficiently   23

             Guide 9   Always Be Courteous and Build Goodwill   28

             Guide 10   Keep Up with Trends of Writing   30

Chapter 2   Writing Positive or "Yes" Letters   41

Chapter 3   Writing Neutral Letters   65

Chapter 4   Writing Negative or "No" Letters   97

Chapter 5   Writing Interoffice Communications   123

Chapter 6   Job Application Communications   159

Appendix   179

CHAPTER 1

Ten Easy Guides to Better Letters and Memos

Writing good letters and memos is a skill that can be learned and that can continuously be improved. Each person has a unique writing style. The intent of this chapter is to help you improve your writing style by applying basic guides for good letter and memo writing. No attempt will be made to change your basic style of writing.

In this chapter, your main emphasis will be on writing sentences and paragraphs. In later chapters, you will be asked to write complete letters or memos.

The chapter is divided into 10 sections. Each section presents a basic guide, and then gives you an opportunity to apply the guide in a variety of examples.

Performance Goal

Your goal for this chapter is to be able to recognize poor examples of writing and to apply the guides you have learned to improve a series of poorly written sentences which will be given to you. Sentences must be complete and grammatically correct to be considered acceptable. Your teacher will determine whether the sentences you write are acceptable revisions. At least 70 percent of your sentences should be acceptable before starting Chapter 2.

Guide 1 ● Plan Before Writing

Planning is perhaps the most important stage in the entire process of writing a letter. Planning is also the stage that is most often skipped in the letter writing process. Too many writers just pick up a pen and start writing or start dictating before they think through the entire process. Writers who try to plan the letter while they are writing frequently find that they begin every letter with almost the same sentence. For example, every letter written in response to a letter received may begin with the following statement:

"Thank you for your letter of (give date)." This statement may be a good opening statement for certain types of letters, but it may not be effective for other types of letters.

Asking yourself the following questions can help you to think through a letter before you begin the actual writing:

1. What is my target? What am I trying to accomplish with this letter?

Most people have a general idea of why they are writing before they begin writing, but often they have not pinpointed the specific reasons for writing. If you answer the question, "Why am I writing this letter?" with the following answer: "I am writing this letter to answer the letter I received." You have a broad, general idea of why you are writing but you haven't pinpointed the specific reasons. A person shooting target practice cannot expect to hit the bullseye unless the target is clearly in view. The same thing applies to writing. Unless you know exactly what you are trying to communicate, it is unlikely that you will be successful in getting the message across.

2. Who is the reader?

Just giving the person's name doesn't answer this question. What you are trying to do is to visualize the type of person the reader is likely to be. Is the reader familiar with the technical words that apply to the type of business in which you are employed. One printer writing a letter to another printer can use technical terms that apply to the printing indus-

Right on Target

Robert J. Knudsen © 1980.

try and will be clearly understood. A printer, however, could not use those same technical words in writing to a customer who wants to have something printed. Terms that are frequently used and generally understood by people in a particular business are known as jargon. To people not familiar with the business, *jargon* generally means total confusion.

Another point to consider is the vocabulary the reader might be expected to understand. Big words might impress a person, but if the reader does not understand the words, you have not communicated.

Other considerations might be approximate age, rank or position, and the importance of the matter to the individual. For example, the tone of a letter asking a judge or high ranking official to speak to an organization would probably be very formal. The tone of a letter asking a teenager to participate in a fund-raising activity sponsored by a charitable group would probably be very friendly and informal.

3. What decisions must I make before I can answer the letter effectively?

All the decisions need to be made before you begin writing. Psychologically, it is not sound to use the same writing style for positive or favorable decisions as for negative or unfavorable decisions. Once all the decisions have been made, you can decide on the best psychological approach to use in writing.

4. Do I have all the information I need to write the letter?

The letter is far-more likely to be well organized if you have all the information you need before starting to write. If you have to stop writing in the middle of a letter to look for more information, you will probably lose your trend of thought.

5. Do I have a mental plan for the entire letter by the time I start writing?

A letter should be completely planned before beginning to write. Writing is simple once you have gone through the entire thought process.

Application:

You received the following letter:

Route 2, Box 787
Moreauville, LA   71355–1159
November 10, 19––

Sales Manager
Harbison Farm Implements, Inc.
1820 Main Street
Marksville, LA   71351–2515

Dear Sir or Madam:

I have just purchased a Harbison Tractor, Model 2220 and will need to get several pieces of equipment sometime this spring.

Although I will not be buying for several months, I would like information or a catalog now. Could you please send me this information?

Sincerely,

Fred Hess

The general manager of Harbison Farm Implements, Inc. gives you two brochures entitled, "The Harbison, Model 2220" and "Equipment for the Harbison, Model 2220." The manager also gives you a current price list to include with the brochures. The instructions are to invite Mr. Hess to visit the showrooms and to tell him a sales representative will be happy to call on him.

Plan the letter you will write by answering the following questions:

1. Why are you writing this letter and what are you trying to accomplish?

_____

_____

_____

_____

_____

2. How do you visualize Mr. Hess?

_____

_____

_____

3. What decisions will you have to make before answering the letter? Will the decisions be positive or negative?

_____

_____

_____

_____

4. What information do you need?

_____

_____

_____

Do you have it all?

_____

_____

5. Do you have a mental plan of how you will write the letter? Give a brief outline of the letter.

_____

_____

_____

_____

_____

_____

_____

_____

_____

Guide 2 • Use the *You* Approach

Who is most important to you? You are! Most people are concerned first with themselves then with other people. If you receive a letter, are you more concerned with what the writer can do for you or with what you can do for the writer?

Many people tend to read business letters with a "How does if affect me?" attitude or a "What's in it for me?" attitude.

The idea of using the *you* approach is to put yourself in the place of the reader. If you were getting the letter, what would you expect? Putting yourself in the place of another is called empathy.

One very visible sign of the *you* approach is that the pronoun *you* is used more frequently than the pronoun *I*. The first place to check for the *I* approach is the beginning of the paragraphs. The pronoun *I* stands out much more at the beginning of a paragraph than it does if it is buried in the middle of a paragraph.

The use of the pronoun *you* is only one small part of the *you* approach. The major part is the entire attitude of the sentence or letter. The attitude should convey a respect for and a genuine concern for the reader. If you are sincerely interested in the reader, then the *you* approach is very easy to use in your writing.

You Are Number One

© Peter Southwick/Stock, Boston

Examples:

"I" approach:	I received your letter of April 16.
"You" approach:	Thank you for your letter of April 16.
"I" approach:	We pay $4 an hour.
"You" approach:	You earn $4 an hour.
"I" approach:	I have scheduled a meeting for 2 o'clock on January 25. Can you meet with me then?
"You" approach:	Would 2 o'clock on January 25 be a convenient time for you to meet with me?

The first examples are primarily a change in pronoun from *I* to *you*. The last example is a change in attitude. In the *I* approach, you have already scheduled the meeting; and the second sentence seems to be an afterthought confirming that you will be there. The *you* approach example is more open and considerate of the reader.

Application:

I. Rewrite the following sentences so that they will use the *you* approach.

1. I invite you to attend a special reception we are sponsoring.

_____

_____

2. We pay 5¾ percent interest on passbook savings accounts.

_____

_____

3. I would like to have a copy of your latest catalog.

_____

_____

4. I am sending you a copy of our new brochure.

_____

_____

5. I have added your name to our mailing list.

_____

_____

6. I opened your charge account so you can use it immediately.

_____

_____

7. We are open for shopping until 9:00 p.m.

_____

_____

8. I would like to have a copy of your report.

_____

_____

9. I wish to express my appreciation to you for participating in our seminar.

_____

_____

10. I want to meet with you at 10 o'clock tomorrow if it is possible.

_____

_____

II. Rewrite the following paragraphs to incorporate the *you* approach.

1. I want to nominate you to serve as Secretary of our Association. I hope you will let me submit your name for this important position. I believe you would have a good chance of being elected, and I think you would enjoy working with the other officers. I hope to have your answer soon.

_____

_____

_____

_____

_____

2. I am asking you to serve as coordinator for the Ray Construction Project. I realize that you have been working with the project for some time, and I think you are capable of handling the job. I would like for you to give me a weekly progress report on the project. Unless I hear from you, I am assuming you will take over this project immediately.

_____

_____

_____

_____

_____

Guide 3 • Use a Positive Approach

The power of positive thinking is tremendous. You can accomplish far more with a positive attitude than you can with a negative attitude. Would you prefer to be around an optimist who has a bright, cheery outlook on life; or would you prefer to be around a pessimist who has a dark, gloomy outlook on life? Almost everyone prefers to be around an optimist.

Most people prefer to hear positive words rather than negative words. Yet, it is very common for positive ideas to be expressed with negative words. Some people refer to this as the donut philosophy. Instead of thinking about the good part of the donut, they wonder why it has a hole in the middle and what they missed. It is very common for people to refer to a half glass of milk by saying my glass is half empty. The person who uses a positive approach would say my glass is half full.

Often, the first word a young child learns to say is no. Seldom do young children learn to say yes be-fore they learn to say no. Think about how many times they are told no they can't do this or no they can't do that. It is very easy to slip into the habit of saying things in a negative way.

Many words besides *no* have a negative image. Consider the following words:

blame	damaged	unfortunate
sorry	failure	wrong
fault	prejudiced	mistake
regret	complaint	difficult
failed	disagree	neglect
never	unable	impossible

Each of these words suggests a negative idea. A reader would much prefer to receive a letter with positive words rather than negative words such as those just listed. In Chapter 4, you will learn to write negative letters in a positive style. Even re-fusals can be written in positive terms.

The following examples illustrate how *positive* ideas are often stated in a negative manner.

HALF FULL?   HALF EMPTY?

Examples:

Negative: Please do not hesitate to call me when you arrive in town.

Positive: Please call me when you arrive in town.

Negative: You neglected to give the shoe size so it is impossible to fill your order.

Positive: Your order will be filled just as soon as we receive the size
                   of the shoes you wanted.

Negative: Don't wait until the last minute to get your shopping done!

Positive: Get your shopping done early.

Application:

I. Rewrite the following sentences to make them positive statements:

1. Sara never comes to the office on Friday, but she is here the rest of the week.

_____

_____

2. Why don't you call one of our sales representatives today?

_____

_____

3. You did not indicate the number of reservations you wanted.

_____

_____

4. No one from the Glenn Insurance Company returned the form except Frank Harris.

_____

_____

5. I don't mind accepting the assignment.

_____

_____

6. Mrs. Caldwell is not expected to return to the office before June 10.

_____

_____

7. We do not accept for credit merchandise that has been out of the store for more than a week.

_____

_____

8. Don't use negative words in your letters.

_____

_____

9. Never call Mr. Smith at home unless the matter is urgent.

_____

_____

10. Jane got three answers wrong on a test that contained 100 questions.

_____

_____

II. Underline the negative words in the following paragraph:

Richard neglected to mention to his supervisor, Alice, that he was unable to determine why the project failed. Unfortunately, it was impossible for Richard to check all complaints in the limited time he had available. Rather than admit he could not find the error, he blamed the failure on a defective part in the processing equipment. Richard's supervisor disagreed with him and felt that Richard had neglected his job. Richard regretted his dishonesty and wished he had never sent the prejudiced report to Alice.

III. Rewrite the following paragraph using positive words:

Since you neglected to send us the type style you want, it will be impossible for us to ship the typewriter elements by the date you requested. We regret this unfortunate situation, but it is not our fault that you failed to provide essential information.

_____

_____

_____

_____

_____

_____

Guide 4 • Check for Accuracy

Two aspects of accuracy must be considered—the content of the letter and the technical correctness or mechanics.

Does the letter make sense? In addition to making sure that the ideas presented are correct, you also need to make sure that facts are interpreted correctly. The following situation shows how the same fact can be interpreted differently by different individuals.

Three young women who lived in the same neighborhood received a dozen red roses from their husbands on a day that had no special significance. Here is how they interpreted the situation: The first young woman said, "My husband sent me a dozen red roses. Isn't he sweet and thoughtful?" The second young woman said, "My husband sent me a dozen red roses. I bet he wants something—probably to go fishing this weekend." The third young woman said, "My husband sent me a dozen red roses. I wonder what he did wrong. I hope he didn't bend the fender on my car."

People view the same set of facts differently. It is just as important to interpret facts correctly as it is to present correct information.

A letter that is technically correct or mechanically correct:

Now for Proofreading

1. Has a good appearance.
2. Uses a consistent style.
3. Has corrections made so neatly that they are not obvious.
4. Is free of spelling, typographical and grammatical errors.
5. Is correctly punctuated.

The best way to make sure that your letters are correct is to develop good proofreading and editing skills. Very few proofreaders are able to find all errors by reading copy just once. Generally, good proofreaders read copy two or three times to make sure that all errors have been located.

If you type your letters, proofread the first time while the letter is still in the typewriter. Errors are much easier to correct while the paper is still in the typewriter. If you handwrite your letters or have someone else type them, you still need to proofread them at least twice.

The first reading should be to make sure that the content is correct. The second reading is to locate any mechanical or technical errors. On the *second* proofreading, printers often read from right to left instead of reading in normal fashion. This causes you to read each individual word because the copy does not make sense. In normal reading style, it is easy to skim over words because you expect them to be there. Printer's style proofreading is especially helpful in locating spelling and typographical errors. Always verify names, numbers and dates. Errors frequently occur in name, numbers and dates; and the only way to determine whether an error has been made is to check the copy against the original.

Application:

I. The letter on the next page has a number of technical errors. Read the letter at least twice, and mark each error that you find. Use a dictionary if you are not sure about the spelling of any words in the letter.

II. Remove the Environmental Services Laboratory letterhead on page 39. Type or write the letter correctly on the letterhead provided. Your teacher will tell you whether to typewrite or handwrite the letter.

Guide 5 • Make Your Letters Simple and Easy to Understand

The purpose of writing is to communicate a message; to *express* an idea not to *impress* the reader with the words you use. The objective of clarity in letter writing is not just to make letters easy to understand, but to make them so clear that they cannot be misunderstood.

You can use long words, but if the reader does not understand those words you have not communicated. At best, you might impress the reader with your vocabulary.

Try to read the following sentence:

The recalcitrant, obstreperous students commenced with an interminable dissertation about the eccentricities of the professor.

Chances are you understand the last sentence much better than the first one.

Short, direct sentences are easier to read than long, involved sentences. If a sentence is too long, the reader will probably have to read the sentence more than once to understand it. You should vary the length of sentences to make the letter more interesting, but 17 to 20 words is probably a good, average length for sentences.

Short paragraphs that deal with one thought are easier to read than long, involved paragraphs. A good, average length for paragraphs is four to eight lines.

What does it mean to you? If you are typical, you probably don't understand what the sentence means.

Try to read the next sentence which has approximately the same meaning:

The noisy, defiant students began a long discussion about the teacher's odd behavior.

If you have to deal with a large number of items or with difficult things, number the items, or use tables, charts, or graphs to make them easier to understand.

Compare the following paragraphs:

Sales of Zest Washing Machines were 2,050 units of $300 per unit for a total sales volume of

Environmental
Services
Laboratory

8467 Burnett Drive Baytown, Texas 77520-3197   Personnel Department   713-328-4274

October 6, 19--

Mr. Kenneth Cassidy
8249 Clearview Circle
Dallas, Texas 75233

Dear Ms. Cassidy:

Thank you for you letter applying for a position as a technician
with Environmental Services Laboratory.

Before we can process your application we need additional information form you. Please complete the enclose application form and
return it direct to me.

It will be necessary for your high school principle too send us a
complete transcript of your high school work. Its not necessary
to send scores from standardised intelligence aptitude or interest
tests. We have our own battery of employment tests.

Your adviser at Southwest Technical College should also be asked
to send us a transcript of your work their.

Please have three letters of recommendation send to us. We perfer
that to of the references be from educational institutions and one
reference should be from a farmer employer.

As soon as we receive all of the information, we will schedule you
for two seperate interviews. One interview will be with our
Director of Personal. The other will be with the Head of the
Research and Developmente Department.

Sincerely Yours,

Mary Burge

Miss Mary Burge
Assistant Director

rg

Enclosures

13

$615,000 for the month of June. Sales for July were 1,900 units at $310 for a total sales volume of $589,000. In August, sales were 2,060 units at $310 for a total sales volume of $638,600.

The information in the above paragraph is hard to understand and to compare for the three months involved. Putting the same information in a table makes it much easier to understand.

Sales Volume for ZEST WASHING MACHINES
June, July, August

Month	Number of Units	Price	Sales Volume
June	2,050	$300	$615,000
July	1,900	310	589,000
August	2,060	310	638,600

Another way to make material easier to read is to number items when you have more than three or four items.

Compare the following paragraphs:

(a) Please send me information about your company policies toward paying college tuition for full-time employees. I am interested in knowing if you pay tuition to what kinds of schools, for what type of employees, what percentage of the tuition you pay, what grade requirements you have, and are courses restricted to job-related areas.

(b) Please send me information about your company policies toward paying college tuition for full-time employees. I am interested in answers to the following questions:

1. Do you pay tuition for full-time employees?

2. If so, what percentage of the tuition do you pay?

3. What kinds of schools do you include in your tuition plan? (Example—colleges, junior colleges, technical schools.)

4. What grades do you require employees to make in order to receive tuition payments?

5. Are courses restricted to job-related areas?

6. What type or rank of employees are eligible to receive tuition payments?

Not only is Paragraph *b* easier to read, it is much easier to answer.

Application:

I. Rewrite the following long sentences which are difficult to understand. One long sentence may be divided into several short sentences.

1. As you requested in your letter of March 14, we are sending you a copy of our latest brochure; and we also have asked one of our sales representatives to call you so that an appointment can be made to talk with you about some of our new products.

_____

_____

_____

_____

_____

_____

_____

2. I have interviewed the two people you requested, and I will send you the report of my interview within the next day or two so that you will have it before you interview Margaret Ellison on Tuesday and Joseph Wayne on Thursday of next week.

_____
_____
_____
_____
_____
_____
_____
_____

3. An unexpected problem with one of our new plants requires me to be out of town all next week; therefore, could you please reschedule my appointment at any time that is convenient to you during the last week of September.

_____
_____
_____
_____
_____
_____

4. The county agent who serves as regional coordinator of 4-H Clubs has requested that we exhibit some of our kitchen appliances at the Trade Show during their regional conference which will be held on February 7 and 8 in the new Civic Center in Bristol, Tennessee.

_____
_____
_____
_____
_____
_____

5. All employees have been asked to participate in one of the Human Relations Seminars scheduled next week and to let you know which particular one of the seminars they have selected to attend so that you can make arrangements for refreshments and have adequate chairs available.

_____
_____
_____
_____
_____

II. The following letters would be easier to read if they were divided into paragraphs. On each letter, use the sign "¶" to mark the places where a new paragraph should begin.

1.

MARINE RESEARCH ASSOCIATES
2764 Oceanic Drive
Annapolis, MD   21401-2122
301-782-2567

April 10, 19--

Dr. Frank Sharpe, Head
Department of Marine Sciences
Eastern Shores University
Edgewater, MD   21040-3018

Dear Dr. Sharpe:

Could you recommend some of the graduates of your Marine Sciences Program to us. We currently have two positions available. One position is for a marine biologist, and the other is for a technician. The enclosed literature contains information about our company as well as complete job descriptions and a list of the qualifications required. Last year you recommended a number of students to us, and we hired three of your graduates. They have turned out to be excellent employees, and we hope to hire two of your graduates this year. We look forward to receiving your recommendations and to interviewing several seniors in the Marine Sciences Program at Eastern Shores University.

Sincerely,

Robert R. Burleson
Personnel Manager

2.

CREATIVE MEDIA
2614 Indian School Road, E.
Phoenix, AZ   85016-5989

February 7, 19--

Ms. Joanne Miller
3479 Navajo Drive, W.
Phoenix, AZ   85021-1313

Dear Joanne:

Several months ago you wrote a series of spot ads for us. The feedback on these spot ads from our client has been excellent. Recently, we have acquired several new major accounts. One large account wants us to develop a complete advertising program featuring newspaper, magazine, billboard, radio, and television advertising. I know you are especially well qualified to handle this particular account. It is the same type of account that you worked with on your last assignment, and I think you would really enjoy this one. Would you be interested in working with us for about six weeks on the same type of contractual arrangement you had the last time you worked with us. Please let me know as soon as possible if you are available and interested.

Sincerely,

Brian Fisher
Advertising Director

III. Rewrite the following paragraphs. Use tables, charts, graphs, or enumerated items to make them easier to read.

1. Last month was an outstanding month for the Columbia Museum of Fine Art. In addition to the art exhibits, the following cultural activities were hosted by the museum: The Almond Piano Concert on October 2 drew an attendance of 200, the Dickinson Poetry Reading on October 5 had an attendance of 75, the Sculpture Lecture on October 8 had an attendance of 40, the Roszak Organ Concert on October 14 had an attendance of 190, the Matthews Concert on October 18 had an attendance of 210, and the Anderson Violin Concert on October 24 had an attendance of 90.

2. Could you please tell me if any tennis activities are being scheduled by Midtown Park this summer. I am particularly interested in learning if any advanced classes in tennis are being held, who the instructor will be, and how large the class will be as well as the cost of the classes. I also would like to know if any tournaments will be held, who can participate in them, and how do you register for them.

Guide 6 • Make Sure Your Letters Are Complete

Completeness means providing all of the necessary information. Many letters are second letters written because the first letter left out basic information that was needed. Mail order houses have developed special order blanks to make sure that customers provide complete information with their orders. Even with the special forms, customers often leave off basic information such as size or color.

Some letters assume that you will know the information. For example: Please plan to meet with me on Tuesday, April 20 at 3 o'clock. It is assumed that the reader will know where the meeting will be held. The writer may plan to meet in the reader's office, and the reader may assume the meeting is in the writer's office. Both could be sitting and waiting in the wrong office.

Dates are often assumed. For example: Will the project be complete on Tuesday? The reader might wonder whether you are referring to this Tuesday or next Tuesday. You cannot assume the reader will know which Tuesday you have in mind.

The time lag between thinking and writing may cause information to be omitted. In order to make sure that all needed information is included, it is necessary to check letters after they have been written. Ask yourself what information is necessary and then make sure *all* of the necessary information is in the letter.

Application:

I. In the space below each paragraph, indicate what necessary information has been omitted.

1. You are invited to be our guest for lunch at noon at the Beacon Hill Restaurant on Beacon Hill Road. Evelyn Sachs will be our guest speaker. Her topic will be "Developing an Effective Records Management System."

   _____

   _____

2. Benito Lopez is demonstrating a new electronic calculator at 10 o'clock on Tuesday, May 10. You or some of your staff may wish to attend this demonstration. It is not necessary to let us know how many will attend.

   _____

   _____

3. Please send me two dozen Super Write Ballpoint Pens, classic style, fine point at $12.50 per dozen. Enclosed is my check for $27 which includes tax and handling charge.

   _____

   _____

4. Would you please meet with us in my office on Thursday, March 17, to work up an agreement to present to Curtis and Associates on the Lindsey Construction project.

_____

_____

5. Please send me two pairs of white canvas jogging shoes, Stock number 67242. Please charge these shoes to my account, No. 437-62-8072.

_____

_____

II. What information must be provided to handle each of the following situations?

1. To order a stopwatch from the Pro Sport Shop.

_____

_____

_____

_____

2. To schedule a meeting of your Social Club in the Conference Room of the Fine Arts Museum.

_____

_____

_____

_____

3. To invite Jane Jarwaski, Purchasing Agent of MTZ Manufacturers, to lunch to discuss the process for submitting bids on a new copy machine.

_____

_____

_____

_____

4. To sell tickets for the Community Action basketball game to help support the Milk for Needy Children Fund.

_____

_____

_____

5. To make a hotel reservation to attend a convention of your professional association.

_____

_____

_____

Guide 7 • Use Specific, Concrete Language

Can you remember the Ivory Soap commercial? Many people who usually pay little attention to commercials can tell you that "Ivory Soap is 99 44/100 percent pure." Specific language calls attention or adds emphasis to statements. Some resort areas are experimenting with specific numbers for speed limits rather than round numbers because

In your own mind, try to specify exactly what each term means in the following sentences. Example: Jerry received a *good* return on his investment. What is a good return—is it 5 percent, 10 percent, or 15 percent? Good does not mean the same to everybody.

of the emphasis and attention specific numbers get. The speed limit may be posted at 43 miles per hour and when the speed is reduced, the next sign may read 37 miles per hour.

Compare your answers to each of the following questions to the answers given by other people in your class or group.

1. Let's go to the Amos Quick Copy Service as I need fast service on this job. (How soon is "fast" service?)

   _____

2. I want to pick up an inexpensive calculator at the Office Supply Shop. (How much is inexpensive?)

   _____

3. Please give me a short report on the status of the Water Purification Project. (How long is a "short" report?)

   _____

4. The majority of students in the small university are employed on a part-time basis. (Majority could mean anything from 51 percent to 100 percent. What percentage? How large is a small university?)

   _____

5. Please send me a copy of the minutes as soon as possible (How fast should you expect to receive the minutes?)

   _____

6. Henry earns a good salary. (How much is a good salary?)

   _____

If you compare the answers given by ten different people, you may get ten different answers. This is the problem with writing in broad, general terms. Simple words may mean one thing to one person and something entirely different to another person. The six items just presented are not confusing when specific language is used. Compare the two sets of sentences.

1. Let's go to the Amos Quick Copy Service as I need 24-hour service on this job.

2. I want to pick up a $20-$30 calculator at the Office Supply Shop.

3. Please give me a one-page report on the status of the Water Purification Project.

4. Approximately 60 percent of the 5,000 students at the University are employed on a part-time basis.

5. Please send me a copy of the minutes within 10 days.

6. Henry earns a salary of $20,000 per year.

Specific language helps the reader to determine exactly what you mean. It eliminates the guess work in interpreting someone else's use of words.

Application:

Underline the general or vague words in each sentence. Then rewrite the sentences in the space provided. Change general or vague words to more specific language.

1. Let's get together before too long to plan another fishing trip.

   _____

   _____

2. Cliff receives a low salary for his work as a keypunch operator.

   _____

   _____

3. Carol receives an excellent rate of interest on her certificates of deposit.

   _____

   _____

4. We need a short meeting to complete the report.

   _____

   _____

5. Doris is a long-distance runner.

   _____

   _____

6. Gregg takes a short walk for exercise at lunchtime.

   _____

   _____

7. James bought a cheap jacket to wear on the camping trip.

   _____

   _____

8. Lorraine had good grades on this report card.

_____

_____

9. The accident did minor damage to Ed's motorcycle.

_____

_____

10. The room will accommodate a large group.

_____

_____

11. Julian was driving too fast when the police officer stopped him.

_____

_____

12. The temperature dropped very low last night, but it warmed up considerably today.

_____

_____

13. The water in the river is rather shallow at this time of the year.

_____

_____

14. Yoko bought a very old car.

_____

_____

15. The store stays open quite late on weekdays.

_____

_____

GUIDE 8 • Use Words Efficiently

Efficient word usage means saying everything that needs to be said and nothing more. Letters need to be concise, but conciseness is not the same as being short or brief. A ten-page letter is a long letter; but if everything in it needs to be said, it is also concise. A 150-word letter may be short; but if it could have been said in 100 words, it is a wordy letter. Letters need to be long enough to cover the subject thoroughly, but short enough to be interesting. Many letters are too long, and contain a number of words that add little or nothing to the message.

Several techniques can be used to make more efficient use of words.

THROW OUT UNNECESSARY WORDS!!!

~~The process of~~ ᴇditing involves removing
~~all those~~ unnecessary words which take
~~large amounts of extra~~ space, but add
nothing ~~of any real significance~~ to the
~~meaning of the~~ message.

1. Use action verbs to cut down on inefficient words and to add more impact to your letters.

Examples:

	Action Verb
a. take into consideration	consider
b. made an announcement	announce
c. send an invitation	invite
d. bring to a conclusion	conclude
e. make a decision	decide
f. make your selection	select
g. make an effort	try
h. give encouragement	encourage
i. be of assistance	assist
j. are of the belief	believe

Compare the following sentences.

1. (a) Please take into consideration all factors before making a decision.
   (b) Please consider all factors before deciding.

2. (a) Please send an invitation to each member.
   (b) Please invite each member.

3. (a) Please make an effort to be of assistance to the committee members.
   (b) Please try to assist the committee members.

2. Replace phrases or groups of words with more efficient words.

Examples:

a. due to the fact that	since, because
b. at the present time	now
c. in the amount of	for
d. in the event of	if
e. in the near future	soon
f. in the majority of instances	usually
g. in a satisfactory manner	satisfactorily
h. on the occasion of	when
i. during the time that	while
j. with reference to	about

Compare the following sentences.

1. (a) Due to the fact that it snowed heavily, classes were canceled.
   (b) Because it snowed heavily, classes were canceled.

2. (a) David requested a check in the amount of $20.
   (b) David requested a check for $20.

3. (a) We hope to see you in the near future.
   (b) We hope to see you soon.

3. Use only necessary modifiers. Some words do not need to be qualified. They stand alone.

Examples:

Use	Meaning	Do Not Use
a. revert	go back	revert back
b. identical	exactly the same	exactly identical
c. repeat	say again	repeat again
d. facts	true statements	true facts
e. maximum	greatest number possible	maximum possible
f. innovation	new idea	new innovation
g. merge	bring together	merge together
h. expert	qualified person	qualified expert
i. cooperate	work together	cooperate together
j. assemble	put together	assemble together

Another group of unnecessary words used to describe are: (colored part not necessary)

Expression	Analysis
a. round in shape	obviously round is the shape
b. blue in color	obviously blue is a color
c. six in number	obviously six is a number
d. State of California	needed only when state and city are the same such as New York
e. City of Tulsa	needed only when city and state are the same
f. three pounds in weight	obviously pounds are weight
g. North in direction	obviously North is a direction
h. three pages in length	obviously three pages is the length
i. gold metal	obviously gold is a metal
j. 30 degrees in temperature	obviously 30 degrees is the temperature

Compare the following sentences:

1. (a) When Jim gets upset, he reverts back to childish behavior.
   (b) When Jim gets upset, he reverts to childish behavior.

2. (a) Arlene moved to the City of Denver in the State of Colorado.
   (b) Arlene moved to Denver, Colorado.

3. (a) Mike wrote a report that was three pages in length.
   (b) Mike wrote a three-page report.

4. Give alternatives only when they are needed. An attorney writing a will may have good reason for making a statement such as "I give, bequeath, and devise . . ." The words have technical differences that apply to different kinds of property such as personal or real property. In most writing, however, it is not necessary to give choices for legal or technical reasons.

Alternatives: (Choose either one, but not both)

a. power and energy	f. actions and deeds
b. study and review	g. activities and exercises
c. help or assistance	h. machines and equipment
d. report or paper	i. problems and concerns
e. value and importance	j. restricted and limited

Compare the following sentences:

1. (a) The Commission predicted a shortage of power and energy.
   (b) The Commission predicted a shortage of energy.

2. (a) Membership in the club is restricted and limited to employees and their families.
   (b) Membership in the club is limited to employees and their families.

3. (a) Please complete the assigned activities and exercises.
   (b) Please complete the assigned activities.

Application:

Revise the following sentences to make them more concise.

1. Please bring the meeting to a conclusion as soon as possible.

_____

_____

2. We are of the belief that each of you should make your own selection of projects to work on this week.

_____

_____

3. Please give encouragement to all new employees.

_____

_____

4. Maria did not ask us to do anything at the present time.

_____

_____

5. In the majority of instances, Alberto approves travel requests.

_____

_____

6. Yang's work is performed in a satisfactory manner.

_____

_____

7. This job is exactly identical to the one we did last month.

_____

_____

8. The maximum possible we accept is six.

_____

_____

9. Our next speaker is a qualified expert on the topic.

_____

_____

10. The jacket was blue in color.

_____

_____

11. The rug was oval in shape.

_____

_____

12. José bought a gold metal chain for Rosa.

_____

_____

13. Please study and review this report by Friday.

_____

_____

14. If I can be of further help or assistance to you, please let me know.

_____

_____

15. Please make a list of the machines and equipment in your department.

_____

_____

Guide 9 • Always Be Courteous and Build Goodwill

Please and *thank you* are simple words, but they build good human relations. All communications going outside the company should have as a secondary purpose the building of good public relations. All communications that stay within a company should build good human relations. Too often we think of adding the notes of gratitude or pleasant statements only for outsiders. This is the same idea as having "Sunday or company manners." Good manners are needed every day and with everybody.

One caution in expressing gratitude is that *thank you* is appropriate *after* something has been done

not *before* it is done. Be careful not to use the expression *thank you in advance*. This implies that you are asking a person something, but telling the person before the favor is done that I am thanking you now so I won't have to do it after you do what I ask. This is an example of poor human relations.

Being courteous also implies showing respect for the reader and having a sincere interest in the reader. Speaking down to people or making them feel foolish or dumb is discourteous. Many people consider a letter with errors or a poor appearance to be discourteous. Long delays in answering letters are also considered discourteous.

KEYS TO GOODWILL BUILDERS

Compare the following sentences:

1. (a) Your letter of June 10 arrived today.
   (b) Thank you for your letter of June 10.

2. (a) Thank you in advance for sending me a copy of your latest report.
   (b) I would appreciate having a copy of your latest report.

3. (a) If you had followed the directions on the order form, you would have your order by now.
   (b) Your order will be sent just as soon as we receive the billing information listed below.

4. (a) Send us the information by January 15.
   (b) Please send us the information by January 15.

5. (a) Enclosed is the catalog you requested.
   (b) We hope you will find the enclosed catalog helpful.

Application:

Revise the following sentences so that they will build better human and public relations. You may use more than one sentence if necessary.

1. Write and let me know when I may have an appointment with you.

_____

_____

_____

2. Thank you in advance for putting my name on your mailing list.

_____

_____

_____

3. I need to see you next week concerning this matter.

_____

_____

_____

4. You scheduled the meeting on Tuesday, December 5. Since Tuesday is December 4, you obviously gave me the wrong information.

_____

_____

_____

5. Tell Dick that I will confirm the price next week.

_____

_____

_____

6. Stop in at our office so that we can correct the statement.

_____

_____

_____

7. The report you sent is a mess and is all wrong. We need to work on it next week.

_____

_____

_____

8. Why didn't you send the book last week as you promised you would?

_____

_____

_____

9. Go get the form signed before coming to my office.

_____

_____

_____

10. I will tell him to do it immediately.

_____

_____

_____

Guide 10 • Keep Up with Trends in Writing

Most of us are very conscious of changes in styles of clothes and of changes in styles of music over the years. We are very aware of clothes that are out of date because the length of the skirt has changed or the width of the tie has changed. If dancers on television were doing the "Charleston," you would associate the music with a time period of some years ago. The same situation is true with letters. Some language makes letters sound outdated.

Ford Motor Company

Ford Motor Company

Styles Change

A few of the trends that affect writing are:

1. Use contemporary expressions. Contemporary expressions are expressions that are currently used. They are not outdated. A term that is used to apply to an expression which is overused is a *stereotyped* expression. A person who uses the same opening sentence for almost every letter is said to use a stereotyped beginning.

Expression	Analysis
a. attached please find	do you have to search if it is attached?
b. enclosed herewith	outdated—if it is enclosed, it is here with it.
c. pursuant to	outdated
d. with best regards, I remain	outdated and poor grammar
e. above mentioned	stereotyped

Expression	Analysis
f. kindly advise	outdated
g. under separate cover	outdated—indicate method of shipment
h. we trust	outdated

2. Make your writings sex fair. Much of the writing of the past has been biased toward the male sex. Writing should be fair to both sexes. For example, when we write to a company we often use *Gentlemen* or *Dear Sir* even in cases in which the odds are very good that the person reading the letter will be female. The following guides may help in eliminating sex bias.

a. Use titles or words that do not indicate sex.

salesman	sales representative
female attorney	attorney
male nurse	nurse
lady doctor	doctor
serviceman	service representative
stewardess	flight attendant
customer service girl	customer service representative

b. When a person gives a title, use that title regardless of your preference. If the title on a letter is Ms. Anne Devoe, use Ms. even though you may know she is married and even though you might prefer to use Mrs. (Ms. is an abbreviation which stands for either Miss or Mrs.)

c. Encourage all female writers to indicate the title they prefer as a courtesy to persons who will reply to the letter. The typed signature would read:

Ms. Dinah Long or (Ms.) Dinah Long
Mrs. Donna Jackson or (Mrs.) Donna Jackson
Miss Sandy Karvelas or (Miss) Sandy Karvelas

d. Professional titles should be handled in the same way regardless of sex:

Dr. Kelly Corbett	Dr. Robert Wade
Lois Walker, M.D.	Ralph Walker, M.D.
The Reverend Sally Brown	The Reverend Steve Brown

e. Alternatives for handling situation when sex is unknown:

(1) All male company — Gentlemen
(2) All female company — Ladies
(3) Female and male company — Ladies and Gentlemen
(4) Use position titles:
   Sales Department—Dear Sales Manager
   Bank Branch Office—Dear Branch Manager
   Hotel Reservations—Dear Reservations Clerk
(5) On form letters, use terms that apply to both sexes:
   Dear Customer
   Dear Friend
   Dear Associate

3. Use a conversational approach. The current trend is toward using a warm, friendly, sincere approach. Write as you talk. Avoid the stiff, ultraformal approach.

4. Contractions are now acceptable to use. The trend toward informality has made the *occasional* use of contractions acceptable. This resulted because contractions are an accepted part of conversation. Excessive use of contractions serves to distract the reader and is not recommended.

5. Build a human relations and public relations emphasis into each letter.

6. Personalize letters and memos. The use of personal references adds to the friendly tone. The *occasional* use of the person's name in the body of the letter or memo is effective. Overuse of a person's name will often cause a negative reaction.

7. Accentuate the positive. The power of positive thinking is tremendous. Be sure that positive ideas are stated in positive terms.

8. Deal with one subject in a communication. Many companies use some variation of subject filing. A letter or memo that deals with two entirely different topics presents filing problems. For example, in which file do you place a memo that deals with *both* the Parker account and McCoy account.

9. The trend is toward circulating copies of communications. The wide use of copy machines has made it easier to give other people a copy of a letter received. For example, a sales representative may write a letter to a person who requested information. That person may in turn give a copy of the letter to the Department Manager. The Department Manager may then give a copy of a letter to the Vice President. As you visualize your reader, remember that the reader may turn out to be someone other than the person to whom you are writing.

Application:

Rewrite the following sentences to make them sex fair and use contemporary language.

1. Pursuant to your request, I am sending you a copy of the report.

_____

_____

2. Enclosed herewith are the documents you requested.

_____

_____

3. Thank you for your letter of recent date.

_____

_____

4. Kindly advise how you wish your order shipped.

_____

_____

5. The books are being shipped under separate cover.

_____

_____

6. We trust the enclosed catalog will meet your needs.

_____

_____

7. Trusting that we have been of service and with my best regards, I remain.

_____

_____

8. The complete record of the Schultz case is available. In the above mentioned matter, the last transaction was dated May 3.

_____

_____

9. One of our customer service girls will open the account for you.

_____

_____

10. Richard Freeman, a male nurse, was the person who took care of him.

_____

_____

11. The serviceman could not find the problem.

_____

_____

12. The stewardess had to rush to serve all passengers on the short flight.

_____

_____

13. A lady doctor x-rayed his foot.

_____

_____

14. The saleslady was very helpful.

_____

_____

15. I'll have my girl type that for you.

_____

_____

Performance Evaluation: Chapter One

I. (Three points each)

Rewrite each sentence to apply the guide indicated in the heading. Provide any additional information that is needed. Check to see that your sentences are complete and grammatically correct.

You Approach

1. We pay $3 an hour for part-time work.

_____

_____

2. I would like for you to preview the film next week.

_____

_____

3. I opened a checking account for you to use now.

_____

_____

Positive Approach

4. Do not call for an appointment until you have completed the report.

_____

_____

_____

5. Do not sign the agreement unless you are completely sure you can accept the terms.

_____

_____

6. Do not mess up the house because we are having company.

_____

_____

_____

Accuracy

7. The principle at the high school gave the students there report cards.

_____

_____

8. As soon as we receive the from, we well check it's accuracy.

_____

_____

9. Call me it you need extra copies, and xe will sent them to you office.

_____

_____

Easy to Understand

10. The house for sale had three bedrooms, three baths, a living room, dining room, and kitchen as well as many extras and a nice wooded lot, and a large deck.

_____

_____

_____

_____

11. Ruth Dodd's sales this month were excellent as she sold the house on Carter Hill Road for $150,000 on May 2, the house on Shannondale Court for $75,000 on May 5, the house on Birch Glenn Court for $60,000 on May 18, the house on Chimney Hill Road for $100,000 on May 24, and the house on Ash Lane for $110,000 on May 28.

_____

_____

_____

_____

_____

12. Pat requested a schedule of Andy's activities since they would be in the same city, and they may be able to get together for a brief visit if their schedules do not conflict.

_____

_____

_____

_____

Completeness

13. Can you meet with the Planning Committee on Monday, August 6, to revise the report.

_____

_____

_____

14. Please reserve a single room for me. I will be attending the Beta Club Convention.

_____

_____

_____

15. Please send me one red sweater and one blue sweater, Catalog No. 86541. My check for $30 to cover cost and postage is enclosed.

_____

_____

_____

Specific, Concrete Language

16. Keith makes a lot of money working on Saturdays.

_____

_____

17. Joyce works late on Wednesdays.

_____

_____

18. A large group of the members walked the short distance to the building.

_____

_____

Efficient Word Usage

19. During the time you are here, we will visit the zoo.

_____

_____

20. Let's cooperate together to get the report done in the minimum possible time.

_____

_____

21. Judy moved to the city of Detroit in the state of Michigan.

_____

_____

Courtesy

22. Do the report by Thursday.

_____

_____

23. Thank you in advance for getting information for me on the cost of the project.

_____

_____

24. Correct the bill and make Gary sign it before you pay it.

_____

_____

Use Contemporary Language

25. Attached please find a copy of the report.

_____

_____

26. We trust this answers the questions raised in your letter of recent date.

_____

_____

27. This is to advise you that your piano is being shipped under separate cover.

_____

_____

Sex Fair Language

28. Do you know who will be the stewardess?

_____

_____

29. Will you call the salesman for a demonstration?

_____

_____

30. Please call the customer service girl before noon.

_____

_____

II. Plan the answer to the following letter: (Two points each question)

"May I have an appointment with you to discuss the Hudson case? I can meet at any time during the week of June 10."

1. Why are you writing this letter?

   _____

   _____

2. How do you visualize your reader?

   _____

   _____

3. What decisions do you have to make?

   _____

   _____

4. What information do you need?

   _____

   _____

5. Briefly *outline* the letter you would write.

   _____

   _____

   _____

   _____

   _____

Environmental
Services
Laboratory

8467 Burnett Drive   Baytown, Texas 77520-3197

Personnel Department   713-328-4274

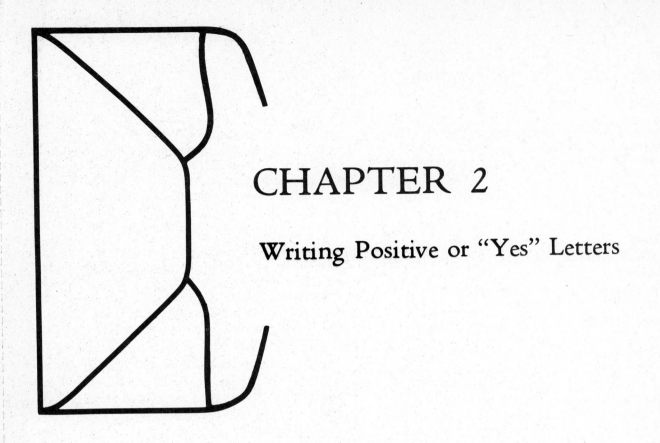

CHAPTER 2

Writing Positive or "Yes" Letters

A reader can generally be expected to react in one of three ways to a letter received:

1. The reader will be pleased with the information contained in the letter.
2. The reader will simply receive the information and will accept it with little reaction. The information neither pleases nor displeases the reader.
3. The reader will not like the information contained in the letter.

The style used in writing a particular letter is often based on the reaction expected from the reader. The ten guides presented in Chapter 1 can be applied to the writing of all letters regardless of the reaction expected from the reader or the style of writing selected. Chapter 2 presents a basic plan for writing letters which are expected to receive favorable reader reaction.

Performance Goal

Your goal for Chapter 2 is to learn to write positive letters following the model presented in the chapter. You are also expected to apply the ten basic guides for effective writing that you learned in Chapter 1.

Preparing to Write Positive Letters

Remember that planning is the most important stage in the process of writing a letter. The five questions presented in Chapter 1 to serve as a guide for planning a letter were:

1. What am I trying to accomplish with this letter?
2. Who is the reader?
3. What decisions must I make before writing the letter?
4. Do I have all the information I need to answer the letter?
5. Do I have a mental plan for the entire letter before writing the letter?

Answers to the first three questions enable you to classify the letter as: positive, neutral, or negative. Once you have determined that the reader can be expected to react positively, then you can begin to formulate a mental plan for writing the letter. A good news letter is easy to write because the reader is receptive to what you have to say. The style of writing can be direct and straightforward. Generally, good news letters are short.

Another reason for following the steps in the model is that it enables you to use the key emphasis locations to best advantage. The opening paragraph and the closing paragraph of a letter generally receive more attention and emphasis than any other part of the letter. The reader is given good news in the two locations that will stand out the most.

Another advantage that results from following the steps in the model is that the writer has a dependable way of getting the letter started quickly and effectively. Usually a letter will flow very easily once the first sentence or two have been written. This is an especially important advantage for inexperienced writers.

The major disadvantage of using the model or formula approach is that your letters could become stereotyped. Stereotyped letters are letters that all begin to sound alike.

With a little bit of care, you can easily overcome the problem of stereotyped letters. The first two ques-

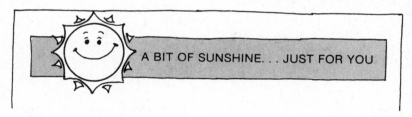

A BIT OF SUNSHINE. . . JUST FOR YOU

Model for Writing Positive Letters

- State the positive news immediately
- Provide supporting detail and any needed explanation
- End with a positive, friendly paragraph

The primary reason for using this approach is that it gives you the best psychological advantage. The main question in the mind of a reader who has made a request is "will I get what I requested?" The main question in the reader's mind is answered immediately and positively. The reader is placed in an excellent frame of reference to be receptive to the rest of your letter. The reader is now free to concentrate on the details of your letter.

tions presented in Guide 1, Plan Before Writing, in Chapter 1 are key steps in avoiding stereotyped letters. The first question was designed to determine the specific objective of the letter. Each letter will have a different objective. Designing a letter to meet a specific objective helps to overcome the stereotyped sound. The second question was designed to get as much information about the reader as possible. The information enables you to custom tailor the letter to the needs of a specific reader. A sincere interest in trying to serve the needs of a particular reader is an excellent guard against stereotyped letters.

Any type of letter that has good news to present can be written following the basic steps in the Model for Writing Positive Letters. Analyze the following letters to see how the steps were applied in each illustration.

Southern Newspapers, Inc.

1867 Commerce Road
Pine Bluff, AR 71601-1614
(501) 723-4567

June 3, 19--

Elizabeth A. Canter, M.D.
Medical Park Clinic
607 Medical Center Drive
Dallas, TX 75235-7981

Dear Dr. Canter:

Presents the good news and makes the request.
The members of the Chamber of Commerce were fortunate to have the opportunity to hear your superb presentation, "The Creative Use of Leisure Time." Many people could use the ideas you presented to enrich their lives. May we share your ideas with our readers by publishing the abstract of your presentation in our Sunday Feature Magazine?

Follows up with needed explanation.
The article would be the lead article and would also be featured on the cover. The author of each article published in the Sunday Feature Magazine receives an honorarium of $500.

Closes with a friendly, optimistic tone.
Our readers will be enjoying "The Creative Use of Leisure Time" just as soon as we receive your permission to print it.

Sincerely,

George W. Anderson

George W. Anderson
Feature Editor

mjw

**Medical
Park
Clinic**

607 Medical Center Drive
Dallas, Texas 75235-7981

June 9, 19--

Mr. George Anderson
Feature Editor
Southern Newspapers, Inc.
1867 Commerce Road
Pine Bluff, AR 71601-1614

Dear Mr. Anderson:

Presents good news ———— You have my permission to publish the abstract of "The
immediately.   Creative Use of Leisure Time" in your Sunday Feature Maga-
                     zine. I was delighted to learn that my presentation at
                     your convention was so well received.

Provides additional ———— The enclosed abstract is a little more comprehensive than
explanation.   the one you received at the meeting. It includes several
                     examples of the projects that were illustrated with slides
                     at the meeting.

Ends on a positive, ———— I look forward to receiving a copy of the Sunday Feature
friendly note.   Magazine containing "The Creative Use of Leisure Time."

                     Sincerely,

                     Elizabeth A. Canter

                     Elizabeth A. Canter, M.D.

mjw

Enclosure

Jordache Galleries

10 Peachtree Square
Atlanta, GA 30340-4677
(404) 254-4704

June 2, 19--

Presents good news
immediately. Even though
the order is not in
the first paragraph,
the first sentence
makes the reader
want to read more.

Mrs. Alyson Cameron
Sales Manager
Delderfield's Art Accents
1058 Madison Avenue
New York, NY 10028-9705

Dear Mrs. Cameron:

The Silverscene advertised in your latest brochure is
exactly the type of artwork we would like to feature in
our Festival of Fine Arts sale.

Presents necessary details
in a straight forward
manner. A positive
approach is used to seek
a solution to the
delivery problem. Note
that an order should
include: descriptive
information, quantity
needed, billing and shipping
information, and delivery
date required.

The delivery schedule in your brochure indicates that six
weeks should be allowed for delivery of the prints. Our
sale, however, is scheduled to begin one month from today.
If you can arrange to have the prints delivered within a
month, please send me 24 limited edition Silverscene
prints, No. 80-J, at $300 each. Please bill the prints
to our account and ship them by air express.

Please confirm this order within 10 days so that the
Silverscene can be featured in one of our major newspaper advertisements announcing the Festival of Fine Arts.

Requests specific action
and at the same time
closes the letter
on a positive note.

Sincerely,

Robert Jordache

Robert Jordache

mj

Note that in this letter the author predicted the reader would
react favorably even though a major problem exists with the time
schedule. The size of the order and the reasonableness of the
time frame provides the basis for the logical assumption of a
favorable reaction.

Delderfield's Art Accents

1058 Madison Avenue   New York, NY 10028-9705   (212) 671-1762

June 6, 19--

Mr. Robert Jordache
Jordache Galleries
10 Peachtree Square
Atlanta, GA 30340-4677

Dear Mr. Jordache:

The 24 Silverscene limited edition prints you ordered will
arrive in time for your Festival of Fine Arts. You and
your customers will be quite pleased with the exception-
ally fine quality of these prints.

By giving your order special priority treatment and by
shipping via air express, we can meet the one month deadline required by your sale. We are pleased that, in this
instance, it is possible to arrange for delivery in less
than our normal delivery period.

Our Advertising Department is sending you today a small
halftone of the Silverscene to simplify the preparation
of your newspaper advertisement featuring the Silverscene.

Sincerely,

Alyson Cameron

Mrs. Alyson Cameron
Sales Manager

rs

Presents the good news immediately. Confirms the order and assures the customer that the selection was a good one.

Follows up with needed detail. Note that the last sentence implies in a positive way that this is a special service that cannot normally be expected.

Closes with a positive, helpful statement.

Application:

I. Review of Basic Guides to Better Letters and Memos

In this chapter, Guide 1, "Plan Before Writing," and Guide 2, "Use the *You* Approach," are reviewed. You may want to review the material presented on pages 1 to 5 of Chapter 1 before completing the following exercises.

Planning Good News Letters

Read the following problems and answer the questions in the space provided.

The local volunteer association has given you the names of several persons who have done volunteer work during the past year. One name you received is Ms. Jill Willis. You want to write Ms. Willis and ask her to assist with a special free blood pressure screening clinic that the local health unit will be conducting at Town Square Shopping Mall during the week of May 10-17. You need volunteers to work from 1:00 to 5:00 p.m. to complete the information card on each person screened.

1. Is it reasonable to assume that Ms. Willis will react favorably to your request? _____ Why? _____

_____

_____

_____

2. What is your major objective in writing this letter?

_____

_____

_____

3. What good news can you use to open the letter?

_____

_____

_____

4. What specific details must Ms. Willis receive in order to make a decision and answer your letter?

_____

_____

_____

_____

5. What ideas can you use to close the letter that will be both positive and optimistic?

_____

_____

_____

Ms. Willis wants to reply favorably to your request.

6. What is the good news that you want to hear immediately?

_____

_____

_____

7. What details must Ms. Willis confirm?

_____

_____

_____

_____

8. What type of positive statement can Ms. Willis use to close the letter?

_____

_____

_____

_____

You are General Manager of Croft Woodcrafters. Mitchell Hudson requested that you come to Albion, Michigan, to give an estimate on building a complete wall unit including a desk, entertainment center, and bookshelves in his office at home. Normally, you give free estimates within Jackson city limits. However, you have decided to drive the few miles to Albion to give Mr. Hudson the estimate which bears no obligation.

9. What will Mr. Hudson want to know immediately?

_____

_____

_____

10. What details will Mr. Hudson need to know prior to your arrival?

_____

_____

_____

11. What type of closing statement would be appropriate?

_____

_____

_____

You are Mitchell Hudson, a CPA. You have decided to have Croft Woodcrafters build a wall unit for your office at home. The unit is to be built according to the specifications and drawing Chalmers Croft sent you. The total price is $5,500, and Mr. Croft assured you the unit would be completed within one month from the time you accepted his estimate. Send a check for $1,500 to confirm the agreement.

12. What information does Mr. Croft want to know immediately?

_____

_____

_____

13. What details are necessary to confirm the acceptance of this job?

_____

_____

_____

14. What type of positive statement would be appropriate for closing this letter?

_____

_____

_____

_____

Use the You Approach

Rewrite the following sentences utilizing the you approach.

15. I would like to have a report on your progress on the XYZ Project on Monday, June 7? Can you meet with me at 9 o'clock?

_____

_____

16. If I see a significant improvement in your performance next month, I will give you a $25 a month raise.

_____

_____

_____

17. I believe I have a good chance of getting you elected.

_____

_____

_____

II. Writing Good News Letters

1. Write the letter to Ms. Jill Willis, 120 Alice Drive, Topeka, KS 66606-7840, you planned on page 47. Use the letterhead provided on page 53. Sign your name as Director of Midtown Health Unit.

2. Write a reply you planned for Ms. Willis on page 48. Use plain paper as Ms. Willis does not have letterhead paper.

3. Write the letter to Mr. Mitchell Hudson, CPA, 609 East Broadwell Street, Albion, MI 49244-2455 outlined on page 48. Use the letterhead supplied on page 55.

4. Write the letter to Mr. Chalmers Croft, Croft Woodcrafters, 512 Mechanic Street, South, Jackson, MI 49203-2250 outlined on page 48. Use the letterhead provided on page 57.

5. Mr. Croft completed the wall unit while you were out of town. Write and tell him how pleased you were with the excellent work his company did. Send a check for $4,000, the balance you owe on the job. Use the letterhead furnished on page 59.

Performance Evaluation: Chapter Two

I. Revise the following statements to incorporate the you attitude.

1. I will pay you $5 an hour to do the job I want done.

_____

_____

2. We ask you to serve as Head of the Business Division.

_____

_____

3. I want to see your results before I leave work at the end of the day.

_____

_____

4. I am enclosing a copy of the report.

_____

_____

5. I pay a 10 percent commission on each sale you make.

_____

_____

II. Plan the following good news letters.

1. Thomas R. Boucher requested permission to participate in a Management Development program at LaGanga Institute. The company has agreed to grant release time from work and to pay the registration fee of $450. A report evaluating and summarizing the program must be submitted to his manager after he completes the program.

a. What good news can you use to open the letter?

_____

_____

   b. What supporting details need to be provided after the good news is presented?

   _____

   _____

   c. What type of positive statement can be used to close the letter? _____

   _____

   _____

 2. You are editor of the *Century 21 Communicator*. You have just reviewed the manuscript entitled "Communicating Without Words" submitted by Dr. Janie Sedgwick and have decided to publish it in the March issue. You need to have a biographical sketch and a glossy picture by January 20.

   a. What good news can you use to open the letter?

   _____

   _____

   b. What supporting details need to be included in the letter?

   _____

   _____

   c. What type of positive statement can be used to close the letter?

   _____

   _____

III. Write the two letters you planned in Section II.

   1. For the first letter, use the following address:
         Mr. Thomas R. Boucher
         29 Sea Cliff Avenue
         Sea Cliff, NY   11579-4008
       Sign your name as Training Director
       Use the Kivett Manufacturing Company letterhead provided on page 61.

   2. For the second letter, use the following address:
         Dr. Janie Sedgwick
         388 Otono Court
         San Jose, CA   95111-6033
       Use the *Century 21 Communicator* letterhead provided on page 63.

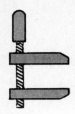

Croft Woodcrafters

512 Mechanic Street, South
Jackson, Michigan   49203-2250

Kivett
Manufacturing Company   52 Independence Avenue   Middletown, NY 10940-9541

Training Department   914-343-2026

The **Century 21** Communicator

8 Linden Place   Cincinnati, OH 45227-1035

Editorial Department   513/232-4380

CHAPTER 3

Writing Neutral Letters

A neutral letter contains information that neither pleases nor displeases the reader. The information is simply received as routine information and is accepted with little reaction. Chapter 3 presents a basic plan for writing routine letters.

Performance Goal

Your goal for Chapter 3 is to learn to write neutral letters following the model presented in the chapter. You are also expected to apply the ten basic guides for effective writing that you learned in Chapter 1.

Preparing to Write Neutral Letters

The same guide you used for planning positive letters can be used for planning neutral letters. Generally the primary purpose of a neutral letter is to convey information. What you are trying to accomplish is to present information in the most effective and efficient way possible.

The more that you know about the reader the more able you are to tailor the information to the needs of the reader. Trying to visualize the reader helps to determine the level of vocabulary you can use, the tone that would be most appropriate, and the familiarity of the reader with the subject. The reader who is familiar with a subject probably will want less background information than a reader who is not familiar with the subject. On the other hand, a reader who is very familiar with a subject may want more technical information than a reader who is less familiar with the subject.

Basic decisions that must be made include what information must be conveyed, how much information must be sent, and what is the best form to use for sending the information.

Once you have determined what information is needed, that information must be compiled. Then a mental plan for writing the letter can be developed.

Model for Writing Neutral Letters

- Present the most important information first
- Follow up with details and needed explanation
- End with a positive, friendly paragraph

Note that the routine letter follows basically the same approach as the positive letter. The psychological reasoning is the same. The reader will be receptive to the information so it should be presented immediately. By presenting the most important information first, you are taking advantage of the key emphasis position. Remember from Chapter 2 that the first and last paragraphs command more attention than the middle paragraphs.

By presenting the most important information first, it gets the most attention. The details which are not as important get less attention in the middle of the letter.

Remember to design the letter to meet the specific needs of the reader to avoid stereotyped letters. Put yourself in the place of the reader and try to develop a sincere interest in meeting the needs of the reader.

Analyze the routine letter on page 67 to see how the steps were applied in this illustration.

The confirmation of Mrs. Roberts' reservation could take several different forms. This is true of any confirmation letter regardless of whether you are confirming a hotel reservation or acknowledging an order.

One alternative for confirming a reservation or an order is to use a printed card with places provided for variable information such as dates. The receipt for a deposit could also be used as a confirmation notice. In some cases, a short personalized letter would be desirable.

In the case of a confirmation for a member of a large group such as convention participants, a simple form letter could be developed. Several types of variable information might be included: type of reservation, dates, and guarantee for late arrival. Using the form is a very simple process particularly when automatic typewriting equipment is available.

Analyze the following form letter. Note that variable information is shown in parentheses. The inside address and salutation would also vary with each letter.

```
Dear (Name):

It is a pleasure to confirm your reservation for a (single room, double room,
suite) from (dates). (Your reservation is guaranteed for late arrival.)

Please present the enclosed confirmation card to the desk clerk when you
arrive. You have been preregistered to simplify and speed up the check—in
procedures.

We look forward to being of service to you and the other members of the East—
ern Information Processors Association.

                    Sincerely,


                    Edward Maxwell
                    Reservations Manager

orp
Enclosure
```

SHARPE INFORMATION SERVICES
14780 CROSS FOX LANE   COLUMBIA, MARYLAND 21044-2058

September 20, 19--

Mountain View Inn
Attention Reservation Clerk
Route 8, Box 415
Elizabethton, TN 37543-8061

Ladies and Gentlemen:

Presents the
most important ——— Please reserve a single room for me from October 8-11.
information   My arrival time will be approximately 10 p.m. A deposit
                   of $40 is enclosed to guarantee the room for late arrival.

Presents additional ——— I am attending the convention of the Eastern Information
detail.   Processors Association which is being hosted by your hotel.
                        The convention rate quoted was $40 per night based on sin-
                        gle occupancy.

Ends on a
positive note. ——— Please confirm this reservation.

                                         Sincerely,

                                         Jane Roberts

                                         Mrs. Jane Roberts
                                         Office Manager

orp

Enclosure

The Information Was Just What We Needed

Using the form just presented on page 66, it is very easy to confirm Mrs. Roberts' reservation as well as the reservations of other convention participants. See page 69.

Another type of letter that is typically considered routine is a request for an appointment. Appoint-ments with individuals in the same city are generally made by telephone. Appointments with individuals in different geographical areas are frequently made by letter.

Analyze the request for an appointment on page 70 and the reply on page 71.

Route 8, Box 415   Elizabethton, Tennessee 37543-8061   Mountainview
Inn

September 24, 19--

Mrs. Jane Roberts, Office Manager
Sharpe Information Services
14780 Cross Fox Lane
Columbia, MD 21044-2058

Dear Mrs. Roberts:

Presents important
information. ——— It is a pleasure to confirm your reservation for a single
room from October 8-11. Your reservation is guaranteed
for late arrival.

Follows up with
necessary detail. ——— Please present the enclosed confirmation card to the desk
clerk when you arrive. You have been preregistered to
simplify and speed up the check-in procedure.

Closes on a friendly,
positive note. ——— We look forward to being of service to you and the other
members of the Eastern Information Processors Association.

Sincerely,

Edward Maxwell

Edward Maxwell
Reservations Manager

fdh

Enclosure

Physical Fitness Center

P.O. BOX 2020   LEESBURG, VIRGINIA 22075-1717

May 20, 19--

Mr. Howard Zimmerman, Director
The Executive Club
1826 Main Street
Hershey, PA 17033-2749

Dear Howard:

Presents the important information. —— Could you schedule an appointment with Ben Cregg and me on either the afternoon of June 6 or June 7? An hour should be adequate for us to discuss the two proposals for developing a physical fitness program for business executives.

Provides supporting detail. —— Our time has been committed for both mornings that we will be in Hershey, but we could come to your office at any time during the afternoon.

The suggestions you made at our last meeting have been incorporated into the proposals. The revised draft will be ready in time to bring with us to Hershey.

Closes on a positive, optimistic note. —— I look forward to hearing from you and hope that you can fit us into your schedule on June 6 or 7.

Sincerely,

Russell Hill

Russell Hill
Director

rr

1826 Main Street   Hershey, Pennsylvania 17033-2749

May 25, 19--

Mr. Russell Hill, Director
Physical Fitness Center
P.O. Box 2020
Leesburg, VA   22075-1717

Dear Russell:

Presents most important information. — It will be a pleasure to meet with you and Ben Cregg at 3:15 on Tuesday, June 6, in my office. The rest of my afternoon is free. We can take as long as necessary to discuss the proposals.

Follows up with needed detail. — Having the revised draft will make it much easier to see the impact of the changes we agreed upon at the last meeting. Hopefully, the proposals can be finalized on June 6.

Closes on a friendly, positive note. — I look forward to seeing you and Ben.

Sincerely,

Howard Zimmerman
Director

eh

Application:

I. Review of Basic Guides to Better Letters and Memos

In this chapter, Guide 5, "Make Your Letters Simple and Easy to Understand," and Guide 6, "Make Sure Your Letters Are Complete," are reviewed. You may want to review the material on pages 13 to 19 of Chapter 1 before completing the following exercises.

Make Your Letters Simple and Easy to Understand

Rewrite the following sentences to make them easier to understand.

1. On Thursday, December 5, a group composed of Jeff Schmidt, Julia Marshall, Tom Schell, Myra Cohen, and George Thomas attended a Personnel and Industrial Relations Seminar in Columbia sponsored by the South Carolina Industrial Board to discuss topics concerned with labor matters, federal legislation, economic outlook, and use of labor statistics.

_____

_____

_____

_____

_____

_____

_____

_____

_____

_____

_____

2. The delegation of students was requested to reassemble and contemplate the advisability and feasibility of developing a strategy for achieving reversal of the unfavorable regulations imposed by the Council.

_____

_____

_____

_____

_____

_____

_____

_____

3. Overall, sales for the year increased with the first quarter sales of $48,000 for small appliances, $120,000 for heavy appliances, and $10,000 for supply items; the second quarter sales of $46,000 for small appliances, $110,000 for heavy appliances, and $12,000 for supply items; the third quarter sales of $51,000 for small appliances, $126,000 for heavy appliances, and $12,000 for supply items; and the fourth quarter sales of $54,000 for small appliances, $130,000 for heavy appliances, and $15,000 for supply items.

_____

_____

_____

_____

_____

_____

_____

_____

_____

_____

_____

Make Sure Your Letters Are Complete

In the space below each paragraph, indicate what necessary information has been omitted.

4. Please be my guest for lunch on June 4 at A.J.'s on Devine Street.

_____

_____

_____

5. Are you interested in participating in the tennis tournament which will be scheduled on six consecutive Thursdays from 6 to 9 in the evening? You can sign up on the first day of the tournament.

_____

_____

_____

6. Please make reservations for the Board of Trustees of the Educational Resources Foundation for lunch at 12:15 p.m. We would like to be located in the private Gamecock Room and have your standard buffet lunch at $5 per person.

_____

_____

_____

_____

II. Planning Neutral Letters

Read the following problems and answer the questions in the space provided.

1. You are Secretary of the Western Consumer Protection Council. You have prepared and typed the minutes of the June 10 Executive Board Meeting. The minutes are sent to Kathy Steranka, President, for review prior to being sent to members of the Executive Board. You have one question about the minutes. You did not get the names of the members appointed to the Audit Committee. You are preparing to write the letter to Kathy.

   a. What is the major purpose of writing this letter?

   _____

   _____

   _____

   b. What other information must you convey?

   _____

   _____

   _____

   c. What type of closing would be appropriate for this letter?

   _____

   _____

   _____

2. Kathy Steranka has reviewed the minutes of the June 10 Executive Board Meeting of the Western Consumer Protection Council. The minutes were excellent. Only one minor error needs to be corrected. The name in the first paragraph on page 6 should be Chuck Sherwood rather than Chuck Sherman. The members of the Audit Committee are: Bob Nesbit, Carol Ruhl, and Ron Sanchez. Plan the letter for President Steranka to Juan Mendez, Secretary.

   a. What is the most important information to convey?

   _____

   _____

   _____

   b. Would it be good psychology to point out the error before commenting on the total quality of the minutes?

   Why? _____

   _____

   c. What other information needs to be conveyed?

   _____

   _____

   _____

   _____

d. At what point in the letter would it be most appropriate to send the additional information?

_____

_____

_____

e. What would be an appropriate closing for this letter? (Hint—What follow-up action should be taken after the President approves the minutes?)

_____

_____

_____

3. You are owner of Todd's Ski Shop. You are interested in broadening the line of ski equipment and apparel you handle. Plan the letter to Treadway Manufacturers requesting a catalog. If the items in the catalog appeal to you, you will consider adding Treadway to the lines you now carry.

a. What is the major objective of writing this letter?

_____

_____

_____

b. What is the secondary objective?

_____

_____

_____

c. What type of closing would be appropriate?

_____

_____

_____

4. Delores Perez, Vice President for Distribution, is delighted to send Todd Cruz a catalog. She also plans to have a sales representative visit Todd's Ski Shop and bring samples of the Treadway line. The sales representative is scheduled to be in the area in approximately two or three weeks. Plan the letter?

a. What will the customer want to know first?

_____

_____

b. What other information does the writer want to include?

_____

_____

_____

c. What type of friendly, optimistic closing would be appropriate?

_____

_____

_____

5. You are Ben Willard, Sales Representative for Treadway Manufacturers. Plan the letter to Todd Cruz requesting an appointment for Tuesday, October 10, at 10:30 a.m. You could also be available at other times that week.

a. What is the most important information you could use as an opening statement?

_____

_____

_____

b. What other information would be of interest to Mr. Cruz?

_____

_____

_____

c. What type of closing would be appropriate?

_____

_____

6. Plan the letter to confirm the appointment with Ben Willard on Tuesday, October 10, at 10:30 a.m.

a. What is the most important information to present?

_____

_____

_____

b. What other details would be of interest to Mr. Willard?

_____

_____

_____

c. What type of closing would be appropriate?

_____

_____

_____

III. Writing Neutral Letters

Each letter should be written on the letterhead provided at the end of the chapter.

1. Write the letter to Kathy Steranka you planned in II-1, on page 74. Use the signature Juan Mendez, Secretary. Address: 318 Broad Street, Seattle, WA 98121-1278. Use the letterhead on page 81.

2. Write the letter to Juan Mendez you planned in II-2, on page 74. Use the signature Ms. Kathy Steranka, President. Address: 1810 Fargo Street, Boise, ID   83703-7123. Use the letterhead on page 83.

3. Write the letter to Treadway Manufacturers you planned in II-3, on page 75. You do not know any individual in the company. Use an appropriate salutation. Sign the letter Todd Cruz. Use the letterhead on page 85.

4. Write the letter to Todd Cruz you planned in II-4 on page 75. The signature should be Mrs. Delores Perez, Vice-President of Distribution. Use the letterhead on page 87.

5. Write the letter to Todd Cruz you planned in II-5, on page 76. Sign the letter Ben Willard, Sales Representative. Use the letterhead on page 89.

6. Write the letter to Ben Willard you planned in II-6, on page 76. Sign the letter Todd Cruz. Use the letterhead on page 91.

Performance Evaluation: Chapter Three

I. Revise the following sentences to make them simple and easy to understand.

1. The enclosed proposal consists of four separate segments, one segment is concerned with developing an employee training package to improve basic English skills, another segment is concerned with developing a correspondence manual, the third segment is concerned with developing a guide for dictators, and the final segment is concerned with developing good form letters.

_____

_____

_____

_____

_____

_____

_____

_____

_____

_____

_____

_____

_____

_____

2. The chairperson of the Board has called a three-day emergency meeting in Boston next week; therefore, it will be necessary for me to reschedule all of my appointments including the one I have with you on Tuesday from 9:15 to 11:30 a.m. Would Wednesday May 6 at 9:15 be convenient?

_____

_____

_____

_____

_____

_____

_____

_____

_____

3. Attendance in our voluntary training seminars has been good for the first quarter; the Time Management Seminar had 12 participants in January, 10 in February, and 15 in March; the Decision Making Seminar had 14 in January, 12 in February, and 16 in March; and the Assertiveness Seminar had 20 in January, 24 in February, and 22 in March.

_____

_____

_____

_____

_____

_____

_____

_____

_____

_____

_____

II. Revise the following paragraphs to make them complete.

1. Please reserve Conference Room A for the Production Staff Meetings on Tuesday, April 6. Ten people will be attending the meeting.

_____

_____

_____

_____

2. Please let us know if you wish to attend the Weight Control Luncheon at noon in the Staff Dining Room. The cost of the luncheon will be $3.

_____

_____

_____

_____

_____

_____

3. Please send a representative of your department to the cost control meeting on Friday, January 20, at 10 o'clock.

_____

_____

_____

_____

_____

III. Plan the following neutral letters.

1. You would like to have Lester Applegate, Coordinator of the Space Management Division, review the draft of the report on space management for your department. Mr. Applegate has been working with you on the project. Plan the letter asking Mr. Applegate to review your report and make suggestions for improving it. The report must be sent to the Space Management Committee within three weeks.

a. What is the major purpose of writing this letter?

_____

_____

_____

b. What other information must you convey?

_____

_____

_____

c. What type of closing would be appropriate for this letter?

_____

_____

_____

_____

2. You are Lester Applegate. Plan the answer to the letter in III-1 of this performance evaluation. You have read the draft of the report. You believe the report is complete and accurate
with one exception. The costs projected should be increased by 10 percent based on new
estimates received from the supplier.

   a. What is the major purpose of this letter?

   _____

   _____

   _____

   _____

   b. What other information must you convey?

   _____

   _____

   _____

   _____

   c. What type of closing would be appropriate for this letter?

   _____

   _____

   _____

   _____

IV. Write the following neutral letters.

   1. Write the letter you planned to Mr. Lester Applegate in Part III-1. Use the letterhead
   provided on page 93. Use the following address:

   Mr. Lester Applegate, Coordinator
   Space Management Division
   Rudd and Associates
   2842 Carter Hill Drive
   Columbia, SC   29206-7012

   Sign your name. Your title is Manager of the Sales Department.

   2. Write the letter for Mr. Applegate which you planned in III-2 of this performance evaluation.
   The letter should be addressed to you. You are Sales Manager of Keystone Electronics, Inc.
   Use the letterhead supplied on page 95. Your address is:

   2846 St. Andrews Road
   Columbia, SC   29210-6601

WESTERN CONSUMER PROTECTION COUNCIL

Reply to: 1810 Fargo Street • Boise, ID 83703-7123

WESTERN CONSUMER PROTECTION COUNCIL

Reply to: 318 Broad Street • Seattle, WA 98121-1278

Todd's Ski Shop
Seven Devils Ski Resort

Route 3   Banner Elk, NC 28604-8120   (704) 963-4373

P.O. BOX 68794
RUTLAND, VERMONT 05701-0051
(802) 876-6788

P.O. BOX 68794
RUTLAND, VERMONT 05701-0051
(802) 876-6788

Todd's Ski Shop
Seven Devils Ski Resort

Route 3   Banner Elk, NC 28604-8120   (704) 963-4373

KEYSTONE ELECTRONICS, INC.

2846 ST. ANDREWS ROAD / COLUMBIA, SOUTH CAROLINA 29210-1852 / TELEPHONE 803-781-3071

SALES DEPARTMENT

RUDD AND ASSOCIATES

2842 CARTER HILL DRIVE   COLUMBIA, SOUTH CAROLINA 29206-2656

803-787-4704   SPACE MANAGEMENT DIVISION

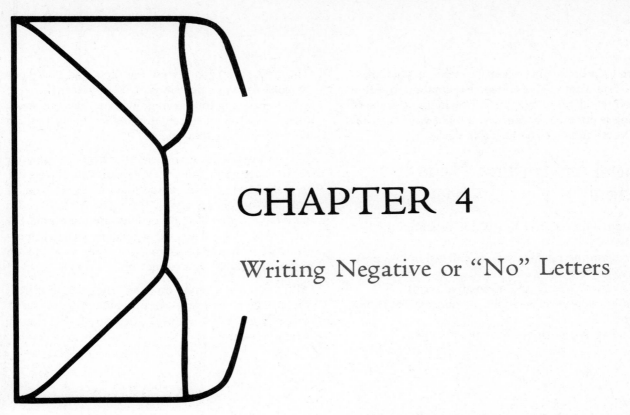

CHAPTER 4

Writing Negative or "No" Letters

A negative letter contains information which is not likely to receive favorable reaction from the reader. In Chapters 2 and 3, the models presented for writing positive or neutral letters were direct and straightforward. Chapter 4 presents a plan for writing letters which contain bad news.

Performance Goal

Your goal for Chapter 4 is to write effective letters conveying negative information following the model presented in the chapter. You are also expected to apply the ten basic guides for effective writing you learned in Chapter 1. You will be given a number of sentences containing negative words and ideas. Your goal is to restate the sentences using a positive style of writing.

Preparing to Write Negative Letters

When you want to communicate information that is not likely to be well received, you have obstacles that you must overcome in order to communicate effectively. No one likes to have requests refused or to be told no. Since the reader will not react favorably to your message, the style of writing you choose must be tactful. You must make a sincere effort to prepare the reader to receive your message. You want to give enough explanation to soften the effect of your message. The indirect style of writing is effective because you build your case before you announce the negative decision.

Model for Writing Negative Letters

- Begin with a buffer to cushion or soften the bad news
- Explain the reasons for your decision in a positive manner
- Say "no" gently and in positive terms
- Offer helpful suggestions or alternatives when possible
- End with a positive, friendly statement

The next step is to review the facts and give your reasons for your decisions. It is important to give your reasons before saying no. The reader is more likely to have an open mind *before* being told no than *after* being told no.

Say no but do not emphasize the negative. If your reasons are good and are explained well, the reader is more likely to accept the logic of the refusal. If you say no before giving the reasons, the reader may have a closed mind or may not even read the rest of the letter. Use as few negative words as possible. It is better to emphasize what you can do rather than what you cannot do.

Although you cannot do what the reader asked, there might be other ways in which you can assist the reader. Offer helpful suggestions graciously when you can.

IF YOU CAN'T ADD SUNSHINE. . .

DON'T MAKE IT STORMY!

Learning to disagree with an individual without being disagreeable is an art. Clients or customers may make requests that are not in the best interest of your business. Although you must say "no" to the request, you value the friendship and patronage of these clients or customers. The style of writing you select must be very tactful to avoid offending the reader.

The buffer is a pleasant or neutral statement that leads to the reasons why you must say no. It is particularly important that the reader is not misled into believing you will say "yes." The buffer enables you to begin on an agreeable note, and it helps to show that you are reasonable and fair.

End on a positive note. The first and last sentences and paragraphs are the key positions that get attention or emphasis. Always save these important positions for positive, goodwill building ideas. Negative ideas in these positions receive too much emphasis.

The letters on pages 99 and 100 illustrate both the direct writing style and the indirect writing style. Although the direct writing style was effective for positive and neutral letters, note that it is not effective for letters containing bad news. The indirect style is much more effective for negative letters.

The same message was conveyed in both letters. The request made by the customer to exchange the

Puzio
609 Fifth Avenue
New York, N Y   10017-9925

June 4, 19--

Mr. Harold Bennett
786 Maple Street
Cincinnati, OH 45230-5525

Dear Mr. Bennett:

Blunt and accusing. —————— We cannot exchange the briefcase you returned
to us for a larger size in the same model.
Obviously, you have used the briefcase for some
time, and it is dirty and worn.

Tone is very bad;
speaks down ————————— We do exchange items when they have not been
to customer. used, but you cannot expect us to accept merchandise in this condition.

Ironic ending;
you haven't ————————— The briefcase is being returned to you under
really helped. separate cover. If we can be of further assistance to you, please do not hesitate to write
us.

Sincerely,

Eva P. Jones

Ms. Eva P. Jones, Manager
Customer Service

cw

DIRECT APPROACH (BAD EXAMPLE)

Puzio
609 Fifth Avenue
New York, N Y   10017-9925

June 4, 19--

Mr. Harold Bennett
786 Maple Street
Cincinnati, OH 45230-5525

Dear Mr. Bennett:

Buffer sets the stage for being fair and reasonable.

The briefcase you returned to us for exchange on a larger model arrived today, and our inspector has checked it.

Gives logical reasons and refuses gently.

Our company prides itself in presenting to our customers only merchandise that is fresh and new. While we are always happy to exchange items that can be returned to current stock, we are unable to exchange items which do not have a fresh, new look. Our invoice indicates your briefcase was shipped over six months ago; therefore, it could not be returned to current stock. The briefcase is being returned to you by United Parcel Service.

Positive close and shows that you expect a good future business relationship.

We are sure you will receive many years of fine service from this top-quality briefcase. A catalog featuring our entire line is enclosed should you wish to order an additional briefcase of a larger size.

Sincerely,

Eva P. Jones

Ms. Eva P. Jones, Manager
Customer Service

cw

INDIRECT APPROACH (IMPROVED VERSION)

briefcase was denied. However, the way in which the request was denied was very different in the two letters. Which one would you have preferred to receive?

The following guides for writing letters containing negative information are suggestions which can help you improve your writing. As you read the guides, pay particular attention to see if the guides were used in the two letters you just analyzed.

No-No's in Writing Negative Letters

1. Don't say no in the first sentence where it will get emphasis and invite a negative reaction.
2. Don't mislead the person into thinking that a "yes" answer will follow. The bad news will be more shocking when the individual finally gets it.
3. Don't begin writing about something remotely related to the topic. The buffer should be directly related to the topic.
4. Don't lecture the person. Do what is necessary to correct the situation rather than telling the person what was done incorrectly. For example: "Please send me the following information so that I can complete your form," sounds better than "If you had read the directions on the form, you would have sent the correct information."
5. Don't use vivid, concrete terms to describe the problem. Specific language makes the problem stand out more. For example: "You obviously cut and damaged the shades when you opened the box." This accusing statement intensifies the problem. Notice how the next statement is less offensive: "It appears that the shades may have been cut and damaged when the box was opened."
6. Don't be curt; but don't overdo the length. Make the explanation long enough to be clear.
7. Don't hide behind "office policy." The reader could care less about your company policy—give a reason. Usually companies establish policies for good, valid reasons. A reader would prefer to know why a negative answer was given. Saying that company policy does not permit something does not tell the reader anything.

8. Don't blame someone else when you are at fault. Everyone makes mistakes. It is far better to admit a mistake and dwell on what you are doing to correct it than to blame it on the computer, a secretary, or someone else.
9. Don't accuse. Accusations force people to defend themselves. One way of stating things without accusing is to use third person, passive voice. For example: "You took the report from my desk," is a strong statement. "The report is missing from my desk," is not nearly as offensive.
10. Don't use negative words. Positive words are more effective.
11. Don't try to give the impression you are bending over backwards. Offer an alternative or counter proposal willingly or not at all. For example, if someone asks for a two-week trial of a new copy machine and you cannot grant it, don't make a big deal out of sending them a brochure with a picture of the machine.
12. Don't repeat the negative or close with a negative idea. Having to say something negative once is bad enough. Statements such as, "Once again let me apologize for the inconvenience you were caused by our mistake," just emphasizes the negative idea. It is better to put emphasis on what is being done to correct a mistake or on the good service that can be expected in the future.
13. Don't over apologize for the action taken. If you make a mistake, an apology is due. However, many times you have to turn down requests, but you do not have to apologize for this action.
14. Don't suggest it might happen again. "If you should have additional problems with your account, please let me know." This statement implies that they might expect additional problems.
15. Don't invite prolonged correspondence. "If you have further questions, please let me know." Once you have said, "no," end the letter positively. If you suggest further correspondence, you will have to say "no" twice. It is much harder to do so the second time.
16. Don't use an ironic ending. If you said "no" to someone and were unable to be of service, don't offer to be of *further* help. "If we can be of further help" could be translated, "We'll be glad to tell you no again."

What is the first thing you notice about these guides? Each guide was stated in negative form. It is easy to get in the habit of telling people what they should not do. Think about each of the guides and try to state each one in a positive style in the space provided below. It takes practice and thought to develop a positive writing style, but positive writing is much more appealing to readers.

In rewriting the guides, it may be necessary to use some negative words. Strive to use as many positive words as possible. Indicate what should be done to make letters more effective.

1. _____

_____

_____

_____

2. _____

_____

_____

_____

3. _____

_____

_____

_____

4. _____

_____

_____

_____

5. _____

_____

_____

_____

6. _____

_____

_____

_____

7. _____

_____

_____

_____

_____

8. _____

_____

_____

_____

9. _____

_____

_____

_____

10. _____

_____

_____

_____

11. _____

_____

_____

_____

_____

12. _____

_____

_____

_____

13. _____

_____

_____

_____

14. _____

_____

_____

_____

_____

15. _____

_____

_____

_____

_____

16. _____

_____

_____

_____

_____

Application:

I. Review of Basic Guides to Better Letters and Memos

In this chapter, Guide 3, "Use a Positive Approach," and Guide 9, "Always Be Courteous and Build Goodwill," are reviewed. You may wish to review the material on pages 8 and 28 of Chapter 1 before completing the following exercises.

Use a Positive Approach

Rewrite the following negative sentences and make them positive.

1. Please do not hesitate to contact us if we can be of further service.

_____

_____

2. We cannot ship your order until our new stock arrives.

_____

_____

3. You failed to mention the color you desire; therefore, we cannot ship your order until you send us this information.

_____

_____

_____

4. Why don't you plan to visit our showroom soon?

_____

_____

5. Smoking is not permitted in this building except in the lounges and in the lobby.

_____

_____

_____

6. Our copies do not have messy ink smudges.

_____

_____

_____

Always Be Courteous and Build Goodwill

Rewrite the following sentences so that they will build better human and public relations. You may use more than one sentence if necessary.

7. Tell Robert to bring the form to me immediately.

_____

_____

_____

8. You spelled her name incorrectly; retype the letter spelling it Smythe, not Smith.

_____

_____

_____

9. Why don't you proofread the letters before giving them to me?

_____

_____

_____

10. You have a problem with the date you scheduled for the meeting. October 6 is not a Tuesday as you indicated.

_____

_____

_____

11. Be at Tim's office before 5 o'clock to pick up the report.

_____

_____

_____

12. Thank you in advance for sending me a copy of your new book.

_____

_____

_____

II. Underline the negative words in the following letter.

November 20, 19--

Ms. Barbara Valdes, Office Manager
Sterling and Associates
1807 Western Road
Edinburg, TX   78539-8760

Dear Ms. Valdes:

It is with a great deal of regret that we tell you we are no longer able to
supply you with custom-made magazine files. Your order was rejected and is
being returned to you.

Because the volume is not high on these custom-made files, it is not worth
our cost, time, or effort to produce them. Why don't you consider
standard-title magazine files? If you do not want to use our standard line,
you will have to locate another dealer which won't be easy to do. You cannot
expect a company to produce these specially made items at cheap prices.

Attached you will find our catalog of standard-title magazine files. If we
can be of further service, do not hesitate to contact us.

Sincerely,

Leon Royal
Customer Service Representative

1. Is your reaction to the letter positive or negative? Why?

_____

_____

_____

2. What could be done to improve the letter?

_____

_____

_____

III. Read the following problems and write an opening paragraph for each one. Remember to use
a buffer—a neutral statement or a logical statement on which you can find a note of agreement—
to prepare the reader for the bad news that is to follow.

1. You received an order for one dozen record albums of the Greatest Hits by the Swingers.
You are out of these albums, and a new shipment is not expected for three months.

_____

_____

_____

_____

_____

_____

2. You were asked to provide an insurance company with the names and addresses of every employee in your company. Your company does not release this type of information.

_____

_____

_____

_____

3. You made reservations for six people to attend a Time Management Seminar on April 20 at Western College. An important company-wide meeting has been scheduled for the same date. You have to write the letter cancelling the reservations.

_____

_____

_____

_____

IV. Planning Negative Letters

Read the following problems and answer the questions in the space provided.

1. You have been asked to participate in the door-to-door collection of funds for the Youth Club on Saturday, March 15. You will be out of town that weekend and will be unable to participate in the drive. Plan the letter to be written to Mrs. Carlota Gomez, Director of the Youth Club Drive. You want Mrs. Gomez to know that you think the Youth Club Drive is a worthy project, and you support it even though you cannot participate in the drive. Is it reasonable to assume Mrs. Gomez will not react favorably to the information in your letter?

a. Why? _____

_____

_____

b. On what points do you think you and Mrs. Gomez agree? _____

_____

_____

_____

c. Can this area of agreement be used as a good buffer to begin the letter? _____

Why? _____

_____

_____

d. What would be an appropriate closing statement? _____

_____

_____

_____

2. You are manager of the Shipping Department of the Atlas Supply Company. You received an order for the following items:

    3 Coat trees
    6 Nylon floor mats
    6 Barrier ropes and posts
    1 Key control cabinet
    1 All purpose engraver

    The first three items are in stock and will be shipped immediately. The key control cabinet is being redesigned to include a more secure wall mounting. It will be two months before the new cabinet is available, and the costs will be $110 instead of $100. A new supply of engravers will be in within two weeks, and the engraver will be shipped at that time.

    Plan the letter confirming this order.

    a. What information will the reader react favorably to in this letter?

    _____

    _____

    _____

    b. What information will receive an unfavorable reaction from the reader?

    _____

    _____

    _____

    c. What logical reasons can you use to convince the reader to wait two months for a control cabinet and pay $10 more for it?

    _____

    _____

    _____

    d. Can you assume that the customer will automatically wait two months and pay $10 more?

    _____

    _____

    _____

    e. Could the issue of holding the order for the key control cabinet be used as an appropriate closing? _____

    How? _____

    _____

V. Writing Negative Letters

1. Write the letter to Mrs. Gomez you planned in IV-1 on page 107. Since the letter was sent to your office, it is appropriate to use your bank letterhead on page 111. Use the following address:

    Mrs. Carlota Gomez
    2700 Chestnut Avenue
    Kansas City, MO 64128-7562

2. Using the Atlas Supply Company letterhead on page 113, write the letter you planned in IV-2 on page 108. Use the following address:

> Mrs. June Schmidt, Office Manager
> Continental Recycling Service
> 8888 Interstate 40, W
> Oklahoma City, OK 73128-9601

3. Rewrite the letter to Ms. Valdez in Part II, page 106, in a tactful, positive manner. Ms. Valdez has been a good customer, and you would like to keep her business. Emphasize the positive aspects of using standard files rather than the negative aspects of using custom-made files. Use the Kuiper and Hudson, Inc. letterhead supplied on page 115.

Performance Evaluation: Chapter Four

I. Revise the following negative statements to make them positive.

1. Our representatives do not call on customers unless the customer requests a visit from a sales representative.

_____

_____

_____

_____

2. Do not cancel my reservation until I confirm my schedule.

_____

_____

_____

3. You neglected to put your identifying number on the form; therefore, we cannot process it.

_____

_____

_____

4. Do not ship our order until further notification as we currently have a shortage of warehouse space.

_____

_____

_____

5. Our company does not discriminate against women, minorities, or the handicapped.

_____

_____

_____

II. Revise the following statements to build good human and public relations. You may use more than one sentence if necessary.

   1. Send me the information no later than March 6.

   _____

   _____

   2. I want an appointment with the general manager before 2 o'clock today.

   _____

   _____

   3. I demand an explanation of the errors you made in my account.

   _____

   _____

   4. Thank you in advance for attending the meeting in my place.

   _____

   _____

   5. You were late so obviously you did not sign the attendance sheet circulated at the beginning of the session. Sign it before you leave.

   _____

   _____

III. Write the following short letters:

   1. You received a request from Mr. Lewis McCann for a catalog. You do not have any copies left of this year's catalog. The new catalog will be available in two months. Write the letter to Mr. McCann giving him the information. His address is:

      Mr. Lewis McCann
      1896 Walnut Way
      Lexington, KY   41018-3211

      Use the Handy Helper Building Supplies letterhead on page 117.

   2. You received a reservation and a $100 check for the Seminar for Secretaries. The Seminar is filled, and you cannot accept any further reservations. Write Miss Ann Johns returning her check and telling her that the Seminar for Secretaries is completely filled. The next time the Seminar will be offered is May 15. Use the Daniel Management Center letterhead on page 119. Use the following address:

      Miss Ann Johns
      6891 Liberty Hill Drive
      Charlotte, NC   28212-5270

   3. You received a letter from Gary Best asking for an interview. He is moving to your city and is looking for a position as a typewriter service representative. You used to maintain your own repair service, but you recently discontinued this department. All equipment is now on a service contract. Write Mr. Best and tell him that you do not have a position available. Use the American Communications Services letterhead on page 121. Use the following address:

      Mr. Gary Best
      2876 N. Michigan Avenue
      Chicago, IL   60611-2307

First
Federal
Bank

10 Pershing Road
Kansas City, MO 64108-3843
816-782-2345

Kuiper &
Hudson, Inc.

2467 Appian Way • Dallas, Texas 75216-2848 • 817-788-8448

Handy Helper Building Supplies

6712 Central Avenue   Lexington, Kentucky 40502-4774

American Communication Services

1765 Rush Street • Chicago, Illinois 60610-3330

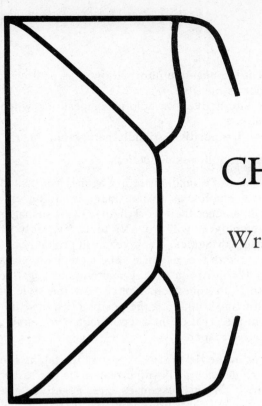

CHAPTER 5

Writing Interoffice Communications

Interoffice communications are communications written to persons in the same company or organization as the writer. The style used in writing interoffice communications is often more informal than the style used for letters. The informal style is used because the writer and reader work together or at least probably know each other.

Interoffice communications are frequently called memos. Several different formats used for writing interoffice memos are illustrated on pages 125 to 126 of the appendix. Memos that are sent to different branches of a company or to persons at a different address generally use a form with a printed address similar to letterhead.

Writing a letter to more than one individual is awkward. The style used for memos makes it easy to write several individuals or a large group of people.

In Chapters 2, 3, and 4, you learned to classify letters as positive, neutral, or negative. These same classifications can be used for interoffice communications. The basic approaches for writing positive, neutral, and negative messages used in writing letters are used for writing memos. Short reports can also be presented in memo style and are discussed and illustrated in this chapter.

Performance Goal

Your goal for Chapter 5 is to apply the models for writing positive, neutral, and negative letters to the writing of memos. You will also learn to write short reports. You are expected to apply the ten basic guides for effective writing that you learned in Chapter 1.

Preparing to Write Interoffice Communications

The same care that is used in writing letters to individuals outside the company should be used to write persons within the company. The memo should be carefully planned, and the information should be presented in an effective and efficient way.

Generally, memos are easier to write than letters. The planning stage of writing is simplified because frequently you know the reader and can adapt the information to fit the needs of the reader. The reader is generally very familiar with the jargon or technical language used in your company. The basic decisions that have to be made in the planning stage are:

1. What information must be conveyed?
2. How will the reader react to this information?
3. What is the best approach to use in sending the information?

Present the negative information in as positive a manner as possible.
Offer alternatives or helpful suggestions when possible.
End with a positive, friendly paragraph.

Consider the following situation:

The manager of a small insurance agency was asked by several employees to consider permitting employees to stagger their work hours. If the manager agrees, employees will probably react favorably. If the manager disagrees, employees will probably not be pleased with the response. The memos on pages 125 and 126 illustrate both a positive and negative response to the question. Notice how the style of the first memo containing the positive response differs from the style of the second memo containing the negative response.

Note that in the first memo, reasons for taking the action are not given. Positive responses are rarely questioned. When responses are negative, the reader usually wants to know why. The second memo clearly establishes that the request was given

Writing the Interoffice Communication

If you expect the reader to have a positive or neutral reaction, use the approach you learned in Chapters 2 and 3.

Present the good news or most important information first.
Follow up with details and needed explanation.
End with a positive, friendly paragraph.

If you expect the reader to have a negative reaction, use the approach you learned in Chapter 4.

Begin with a buffer.
Explain the reasons for your decision.

serious consideration and that the reasons for refusal are logical. The last paragraph is included for human relations purposes.

Using Memorandum Style for Short Reports

Many reports that are short and informal are presented in memorandum style. Reports are tools which help managers make decisions. Usually a report is assigned, and the person who requests the information indicates exactly what kind of information is needed.

 **MIDLAND INSURANCE AGENCY**
Interoffice Communication

TO: All Employees

FROM: Eleanor Bruner

DATE: January 10, 19--

SUBJECT: Working Hours

A plan for staggering work hours has been devised and will become effective on Monday, February 2. Each employee will be able to select from four options, the hours he or she prefers to work.

The options for working hours are:

1. 8:00 a.m. to 4:00 p.m.
2. 8:30 a.m. to 4:30 p.m.
3. 9:00 a.m. to 5:00 p.m.
4. 9:30 a.m. to 5:30 p.m.

It is important that at least two employees be scheduled for each option. The preliminary survey indicated that at least three employees preferred each option so our office should be adequately staffed at all times.

Please let me know within a week which hours you have selected to work. I am pleased to be able to provide alternative working hours to meet the needs of each employee.

fk

MIDLAND INSURANCE AGENCY
Interoffice Communication

TO: All Employees

FROM: Eleanor Bruner

DATE: January 10, 19--

SUBJECT: Working Hours

Several employees have requested that I consider developing a plan for staggering work hours. For the past two weeks, I have been exploring alternatives and assessing the impact of each on our agency.

The lease on our office space here in Midland Executive Park provides heating, cooling, and security based on our present office hours of 8:30 to 4:30. Since all other tenants of Midland Executive Park operate on a 8:30 to 4:30 schedule, the property manager is reluctant to consider renegotiating the lease.

Another consideration is that the Office Manager is responsible for receiving and depositing all funds and for approving special trans- actions. Extended working hours would require significant changes in our current office policies. We have considered adding an Assistant Office Manager to the staff, but the position is not funded in our current budget.

While it is not feasible to offer a plan for staggering work hours now, perhaps some alternative will become available when our lease comes up for renewal and when our budget for the next fiscal year is considered.

I welcome your suggestions for improving the working conditions in our agency and for making our agency more efficient.

fk

Organization of the information presented in the report is important. Summaries, headings, lists, tables, charts, and graphs can be used to organize and simplify the data presented.

The style of writing used for reports is often more formal than the style of writing used for letters and memos. Companies expect reports to be objective. Personal pronouns such as "I" and "we" tend to make the report sound subjective, and generally are not used in formal reports. Reports written in memorandum style tend to be less formal than other types of reports. The pronouns "I" and "we" are sometimes used in these informal reports.

Writing in objective style can be learned with a little practice. Compare the following illustrations:
1. (a) I have completed my study of absenteeism for our company.
   (b) The study of absenteeism in our company has been completed.
2. (a) I found that absenteeism is much higher on Fridays than on any other day of the week.
   (b) Absenteeism in our company is higher on Fridays than on any other day of the week.
3. (a) I recommend that we establish a centralized filing system.
   (b) A centralized filing system appears to be the best alternative.
4. (a) I compared my results with the results of the industry survey, and I found my results to be very favorable.
   (b) The results of this survey compare very favorably with the results of the industry survey.

Contents of the Report

Short reports generally contain the following:
1. Identification. In the memo style report, the printed heading including the subject line can be used to provide the identifying information.
2. Problem. The problem is a statement of the purpose of the report. It explains what you are trying to accomplish.
3. Supporting Information. Data or factual information collected to solve the problem is presented.
4. Analysis. The analysis consists of a discussion of the facts and how these facts can be used to solve the problem.
5. Conclusions. The results produced by analyzing facts and applying the facts to the problem are called conclusions.
6. Recommendations. The conclusions are used to determine appropriate action to be taken.
7. Summary. Reports generally contain a brief summary. The summary may be incorporated with the conclusions and recommendations in very short reports, or presented separately.

Very informal reports may not include all seven items as separate sections, but generally the information will be included in some fashion.

Organization of The Report

Narrative Approach

Reports can be organized in several different ways. One way commonly used is simply to give an account of activities in the order that they happened. Giving an account of activities is an easy way to write a report, but it is not always the best approach to use. Often, it is difficult to compare information or to emphasize information in the narrative-style report.

Direct Approach

A report that is organized using the direct approach presents the main statement or conclusion then supports it with needed details. The direct approach is particularly good when the reader is likely to agree with the conclusion. It is not a good persuasive style. If the reader disagrees with the conclusion, the reader will probably question the facts and object to the way they are presented.

Indirect Approach

A report that is organized using the indirect approach presents the facts and supporting information and lets the facts lead to a logical conclusion. The reader is more likely to read objectively if the conclusion is not known at the beginning. The indirect approach is more convincing and persuasive than the direct approach.

EXAMPLE

Allen Elliott, Office Manager of Biddle, Blake, and Associates was asked to study a proposal from the Scott Company to replace the four convenience copiers currently being used with a new Scott Copier/Duplicator. Corwin Biddle wants a recommendation from Allen Elliott based on a survey of copy needs of the company.

The same information was used to write the following reports. Compare the organizational approach used in each report.

BIDDLE, BLAKE, and Associates
Internal Memorandum

TO: Corwin Biddle

FROM: Allen Elliott

DATE: June 25, 19--

SUBJECT: Survey of Copy Needs

The survey of our copy needs, which you requested on June 5, has been completed. The company currently has two Wilson Copiers and two Mathas Copiers. The average volume on the Wilson Copiers is 40,000 copies per month. The average volume on the Mathas Copiers is also 40,000 per month.

Current costs average 4 cents per copy on the Wilson Copiers and 6 cents per copy on the Mathas Copiers.

Copy quality is adequate, but not excellent. The image of the company could be improved with better copy quality.

The Scott Copier/Duplicator which has been proposed was also studied. The Scott Copier/Duplicator is capable of handling easily the 80,000 copies averaged per month. Costs per copy on the Scott Copier/Duplicator average 3 cents per copy. Supplies are less expensive than the supplies currently being used.

The Scott Copier/Duplicator uses plain bond paper and gives excellent copy quality.

Four copiers make copying more convenient for employees. However, the service on a larger copier/duplicator would be better. Consolidating copiers results in a savings of 900 square feet of floor space.

The Scott Copier/Duplicator is recommended. The advantages and disadvantages of each alternative were carefully considered. The most significant factors are the cost effectiveness and the superior quality of the Scott Copier/Duplicator.

rw

NARRATIVE APPROACH

BIDDLE, BLAKE, and Associates
Internal Memorandum

TO: Corwin Biddle

FROM: Allen Elliott

DATE: June 25, 19--

SUBJECT: Survey of Copy Needs

A comparison of the Wilson and Mathas copiers currently being used and the proposed Scott Copier/Duplicator indicated that the Scott Copier/ Duplicator is the best alternative for the company.

The Scott is more cost effective than our Wilson and Mathas copiers. The costs are:

COPIER	AVERAGE MONTHLY VOLUME	AVERAGE COST PER COPY
Wilson Copier	40,000	4 cents
Mathas Copier	40,000	6 cents
Scott Copier/Duplicator	80,000	3 cents

Supplies for the Scott Copier/Duplicator will also be less expensive than the supplies currently used with the Wilson and Mathas copiers.

A comparison of copy quality showed that the Scott copies are significantly better than either the Wilson or Mathas copies. The Scott uses plain bond paper rather than the special paper used in the Wilson and Mathas copiers.

Convenience to employees was another consideration. The convenience of having four copiers at different locations will probably be offset by the better service which can be provided by the Scott Copier/Duplicator. Using one copier instead of four will save 900 square feet of floor space.

The Scott Copier/Duplicator is recommended. The advantages were carefully considered. The most significant factors are the cost effectiveness and the superior quality of the Scott Copier/Duplicator.

rw

DIRECT APPROACH

BIDDLE, BLAKE, and Associates
Internal Memorandum

TO: Corwin Biddle

FROM: Allen Elliott

DATE: June 25, 19--

SUBJECT: Survey of Copy Needs

A number of factors were considered in comparing the Wilson and Mathas copiers currently being used with the proposed Scott Copier/Duplicator.

Comparative copy costs are:

	AVERAGE MONTHLY VOLUME	AVERAGE COST PER COPY
Wilson Copier	40,000	4 cents
Mathas Copier	40,000	6 cents
Scott Copier/Duplicator	80,000	3 cents

The average cost per copy of the Scott Copier/Duplicator is less than the average cost per copy on the copiers currently being used. Supplies are also less expensive.

A comparison of copy quality was also made. Copies made on the Scott copier are made on bond paper whereas the Wilson and Mathas copiers use special paper. Copies made on the Scott Copier/Duplicator are significantly better than copies made on either the Wilson or the Mathas copiers.

Having four copiers is more convenient for employees than having one copier would be. However, a larger copier/duplicator would provide better service. The four copiers currently occupy 900 more square feet of floor space than would be required for the Scott Copier/Duplicator.

The Scott Copier/Duplicator is recommended. The advantages and disadvantages of each alternative were carefully considered. The significant factors are the cost effectiveness and the superior quality of the Scott Copier/Duplicator.

rw

INDIRECT APPROACH

Comparison of Organizational Approaches

The narrative style simply gives a chronological report of the action taken and the results obtained. It is difficult to compare the present copiers with the proposed copier because the information is contained in different paragraphs. The reader will probably have to go back and read the information a second time to make the comparisons. The first paragraph—a key emphasis position—was used to present trivia. The first things done were not the most important.

The direct style is excellent if the reader agrees with the conclusion contained in the first paragraph. The reader who disagrees with the conclusion is not likely to read with an open mind. In fact, the reader will probably be trying to find fault with the reasoning used to justify the conclusion.

The indirect style is particularly good if the reader disagrees with the conclusion. Since the reader does not know what the conclusion will be, the reader is more likely to be objective in analyzing the facts presented. The indirect style uses an objective analysis of facts to lead to a logical conclusion.

Application:

I. Review of Basic Guides to Better Letters and Memos

In this chapter, Guide 4, "Check for Accuracy," and Guide 7, "Use Specific, Concrete Language," are reviewed. You may wish to review the material on pages 10 and 21 of Chapter 1 before completing the following exercises.

Check for Accuracy

Circle the errors in the following paragraphs:

1. A good employee benefit program is a positive force in helping too recruit new employs. Companys with outstanding benefit programs often have low turnover and absenteeism rates.
2. Many efforts are being made two increase productivity of office workers. Factory work is much easier to measure than office word. Most of the attention is being payed to clerical and secretarial functions. Little have been done to improve the productivity of management.
3. Letters can make either a good or a bad impression. A letter with spelling typographical or grammatical errors are a sign of indifference or incompetence. Proofread careful to detect all errors.

Use Specific, Concrete Language

Rewrite the following sentences changing general words to more specific language.

4. The raincoat was very expensive.

_____

_____

5. The water in Lake Murray is very deep.

_____

_____

6. My car is not very old.

_____

_____

7. A long report will take too much time to prepare.

_____

_____

8. Will you take a short walk with me?

_____

_____

II. Planning Interoffice Communications

Read the following problems and answer the questions in the space provided.

1. You are Danny Taylor, a sales representative for Casual Style Furniture Company. Yesterday, you sold two sets of the new Casual Elegance line of patio furniture. According to inventory records, ten sets were available in the warehouse. You promised customers delivery within a day or two. However, when you called the warehouse to schedule the deliveries, the clerk indicated the furniture was out of stock and would have to be ordered. Joe, the other sales representative who works with you, had the same problem with other lines of patio furniture. Plan a memo to the warehouse supervisor, Walter Allman, and ask that the stock of all patio furniture be verified and a new inventory report be sent to the store as soon as possible.

a. How do you expect Walter to react to your memo? _____

_____

_____

Why? _____

_____

b. Would it be better to explain the problems you are having or just request a new inventory
    record? _____

_____

_____

Why? _____

_____

c. Is a buffer necessary or desirable in this case?_____Why? _____

_____

_____

d. What types of closing would be appropriate?_____

_____

_____

2. You are Walter Allman, Warehouse Supervisor. After checking the warehouse records and stock of patio furniture, you discovered that data from an outdated record was sent to the store in error. Plan the memo to Joe Greene and Danny Taylor sending a corrected inventory report.

a. How do you expect Joe and Danny to react?

_____

_____

Why? _____

_____

b. Would it be desirable to explain the reasons for the incorrect report?

_____

_____

Why? _____

_____

c. Is a buffer needed for this letter? _____ Why? _____

_____

d. What type of closing would be appropriate?

_____

3. You are Supervisor of the Reprographics Center. You have just purchased a large copier/ duplicator for the center. The new equipment will enable you to improve service and copy quality significantly. The equipment will be installed on Thursday and Friday of next week. The Reprographics Center will not be able to provide any service during the two days of installation. A small convenience copier is available in the mail room for emergency work. Plan the memo to notify all employees about the purchase of the equipment and the two days of downtime.

a. Can the readers be expected to react favorable or unfavorably to this memo?

Why? _____

_____

b. The memo contains both good news (the purchase of new equipment) and bad news (two days of downtime while the machine is being installed). Which approach would be best to use in this case?

_____

_____

Why? _____

_____

c. Outline the information that should be presented.

_____

_____

_____

_____

4. You have been asked to update the company directory of all employees. The directory contains the following information:
   Employee's name, office number, and telephone number
   Home address and telephone number
   Spouse's name and names of children
   Each employee receives a copy of the directory. Plan a memo to all employees asking each one to verify the information that is currently in the directory and requesting any changes that should be made. Also plan a return form for providing the needed information.

   a. Would it be better to ask every employee to return the form or to ask those employees with changes in the data to return the form? _____

   Why? _____

   _____

   _____

   b. Should a deadline for returning the form be given?_____

   Why? _____

   _____

   _____

   c. Why is it better to send a form rather than to ask each one to notify you of changes?

   _____

   _____

   d. What information should be included on the form? _____

   _____

   _____

5. Plan a follow-up memo to employees who did not respond to the memo you planned in Problem 4.

   a. Should another form be sent?_____ Why? _____

   _____

   _____

   b. What type of information should be included? _____

   _____

III. Writing Interoffice Communications

1. Write the memo to Walter Allman that you (Danny Taylor) planned in II-1 on page 132. Use the form provided on page 139.
2. Write the memo to Joe Greene and Danny Taylor you (Walter Allman) planned in II-2 on page 132. Only one memo needs to be written, but both sales representatives should receive a copy of it. Use the form furnished on page 141.
3. Write the memo you (the Supervisor) planned in Part II-3 on page 133. It should be addressed to all employees from you. Use the form supplied on page 143.
4. Write the memo you planned in Part II-4, page 134. Address it to all employees from you. Design the form to be sent. The form may be placed either on the bottom of the memo or on a separate sheet of paper. Use the memo form on page 145.
5. Write the memo you planned in II-5, on page 134. Use the form on page 147.

IV. Writing in Objective Style

Rewrite the following sentences to eliminate the personal pronouns "I" and "we."

1. I compared the size of the new rug to the old rug, and I found the new one to be six inches longer.

   _____

   _____

2. I analyzed the quality of both types of paper, and I think the quality is about the same.

   _____

   _____

3. Before we reviewed the new proposal, we studied our current situation.

   _____

   _____

4. I found our current inventory of calculators to be 28.

   _____

5. Mr. Riggs requested that I have the report ready by Friday if I possibly can.

   _____

   _____

V. Writing Short Reports

Read the following problems. Then plan and write the report required.

1. Mrs. Felicia Navarro, Training Manager, asked you to study the registration list from yesterday's voluntary Time Management Seminar sponsored by the Training Department. She wants to know what type of employees are attending the seminar. The information you provide will be used in making decisions on the type of promotion to use for the next seminar. You analyzed the registration forms and came up with the following information.

   a. All four departments were represented:
      Accounting—4 people out of 9
      Production— 8 people out of 14
      Sales—7 people out of 11
      Administration—12 people out of 18

   b. Both male and female employees participated in the program:
      Male—17 out of 30
      Female—14 out of 22

   c. Employees were from a variety of positions:
      Managers—7 out of 14
      Secretaries—8 out of 13
      Sales Representatives—6 out of 9
      Accountants—4 out of 6

   When you compared the number possible in each department and group, you found that you had good representation in each case. You concluded that no pattern of attendance could be determined. For this report, use the memo form on page 149.

2. You are Supervisor of Centralized Supplies. Recently, you have been having problems with a shortage of paper supplies. Your manager has asked you to send a status report to each

manager indicating the current status of supplies. The style can be very informal. Personal pronouns may be used. Use the interoffice memo form on page 151.

You have updated your inventory records, but you have decided that the inventory records would not be very meaningful to any of the managers. Very few managers would know how long 20 cartons of paper could be expected to last. Therefore, you decided to convert that information to average week's supply. The inventory record will be an attachment to your report.

Product	Supply on Hand	Expected Shipment Date	Supply Expected
Letterhead	6 weeks	10-15 days	6 weeks
Paper for copier	1 week	10-15 days	4 weeks
Computer paper	1 week	6- 8 days	2 weeks
Bond paper	3 weeks	15 days	6 weeks
Card stock	out	10 days	6 weeks
Envelopes	10 weeks	6 days	12 weeks

You want to make it clear that adequate paper supplies have been ordered, but because of the shortage of paper, suppliers notified you of revised shipment dates. You feel sure the expected dates shown in the chart are realistic. It is important to warn managers to conserve supplies so that the total supply will not be consumed before the new supply arrives.

Performance Evaluation: Chapter Five

I. Correct the errors in the following paragraph:

The open-plan office has many advantages over the traditional office. Its cheaper, easier to make changes, and require less space. However it also has disadvantages. Security and noise are the major problems. Also, many employees like the status than is often attach to a private office. Open-plan offices can be both attractive and functional.

II. Rewrite the following sentences using specific, concrete language.

1. Interest rates on home mortgages are extremely high.

   _____

   _____

   _____

2. The room will accommodate a large group, but it will take a while before it can be set up.

   _____

   _____

   _____

3. She was traveling at a high rate of speed when the accident occurred, but did only minor damage to her motorcycle.

   _____

   _____

   _____

4. Eric waited a long time for a taxi to travel such a short distance.

_____

_____

_____

III. Plan and write the following interoffice memos:

1. Notify all employees that a new, variable holiday has been added to this year's schedule of holidays given by the company. Employees will be given a paid holiday on their birthday. This day was granted in appreciation of the outstanding efforts of employees in making last year a record year in production and in sales. Use the interoffice memo form provided on page 153.
2. Write all employees informing them that no vacations may be scheduled during the last two weeks of June. This policy exists because of the tremendous volume of work involved in closing out the fiscal year. Use the interoffice memo form on page 155.

IV. Plan and write the following short report. Use the interoffice memo form provided on page 157.

As production manager, you prepare a report on the 15th of each month giving the status of major projects. In this report, you notify supervisors of projects that may be behind schedule and might require overtime.

Here is the current status of your major projects:

Project A201, the Fernandez account, is due October 20. It has already been printed.

Project A206, the Wooden account, is due October 24. It has been type set.

Project C202, the Kane account, is due October 28. It has not been touched.

Project B207, the Hollingsworth account, is due October 18. It has been collated and stapled.

Project A209, the Oxford account, is due November 2. The halftones are ready.

Project B211, the Peake account, is due November 6. It has not been touched.

Project C213, the Roof account, is due November 3. It has been printed.

Project B215, the Karandisevsky account, is due November 15. It has not been touched.

Three of these projects are significantly behind schedule and may require overtime to complete them: C202, A209, and B211.

Casual Style **Furniture Company**   **MEMORANDUM**

TO:

FROM:

DATE:

SUBJECT:

Casual Style Furniture Company

MEMORANDUM

TO:

FROM:

DATE:

SUBJECT:

STATE OF TENNESSEE
Department of Health and Environmental Control

220 Public Square
Nashville, Tennessee 37201-6372

Memorandum

TO:

FROM:

DATE:

SUBJECT:

O'HARA-PHILLIPS

Memorandum

TO:

FROM:

DATE:

SUBJECT:

O'HARA-PHILLIPS

Memorandum

TO:

FROM:

DATE:

SUBJECT:

Oar Continental Company

Training Department   Memorandum

TO:

FROM:

DATE:

SUBJECT:

Sterling Trucking Company
1090 Pelham Road
New York, NY 10805-9229
212-672-4634

Interoffice Memorandum

TO:

FROM:

DATE:

SUBJECT:

Super T Manufacturing Company

Office of the President

TO:

FROM:

DATE:

SUBJECT:

BRIAN SPECIALTY COMPANY
820 Main Street
Wilson, North Carolina 27983-9171
919-291-7245

MEMORANDUM

TO:

FROM:

DATE:

SUBJECT:

MIDWESTERN PRINTERS, Inc.

Production Department   **Memorandum**

TO:

FROM:

DATE:

SUBJECT:

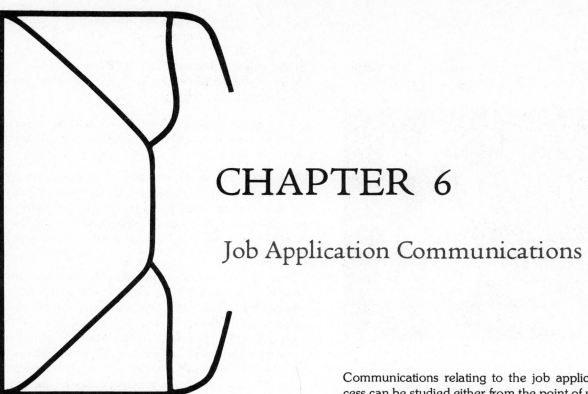

CHAPTER 6

Job Application Communications

Communications relating to the job application process can be studied either from the point of view of the individual trying to get a job or from the point of view of the employer trying to hire an employee. A letter that is effective for a person trying to get a job will also be effective from the viewpoint of the employer hiring an employee.

A number of different types of communications are included in the job application process. Job application communications covered in this chapter include: application letter, resume, application form, request for recommendation, and recommendation letter.

Performance Goal

Your goal for Chapter 6 is to write effective job application communications. You are also expected to apply the ten basic guides for effective writing that you learned in Chapter 1.

Job Application Letters

The application letter may or may not be a part of the job application process. Many individuals obtain jobs without ever writing an application letter. Jobs which are obtained without a letter of application are generally advertised on the open market. Usually notice of the jobs is placed in the classified ads of a newspaper or professional journal, or they are posted with a placement or government agency. The hiring process often consists of a telephone call, completion of an application form, a screening interview, and possibly a follow-up interview.

Applying for a Job

Many jobs require an application letter. Some classified ads specifically request an application letter and give the address. Persons desiring to move to another city usually have to write application letters. The greatest number of application letters are probably written to obtain unadvertised jobs. Estimates indicate that the number of unadvertised jobs may be at least two or three times greater than the number of advertised jobs.

The best sources for learning about unadvertised jobs are: well-informed people in the field, employees of a company, and personnel departments or individuals with the authority to hire in a company. For example, a business teacher may know of several secretarial, sales, or accounting jobs available.

Employees may know of jobs that will become available in their companies in the near future. Many companies develop the reputation of being a good company to work for, and as a result receive many applications based on the hope that a job will become available soon.

Finding a suitable job requires careful planning and hard work. The individual who searches only advertised sources may miss out on the best job opportunities. The individual who is willing to search for the best possible job may create a number of desirable alternatives.

The job application letter is often a transmittal letter or cover letter for a resume. The resume, some-times called a personal data sheet or vita, is a summary of the qualifications and experience that qualify an individual for a job.

Planning is a key part of the job application process. Self-analysis is a prerequisite to writing either the letter or the resume.

The first step is to evaluate your strengths and weaknesses. It is important to take an objective look at the strengths you possess that will help you get a job. It is also equally important to look objectively at the weaknesses that might hinder you in getting a job.

Once you have analyzed yourself, you can then begin to analyze jobs. Seek to find the type of job that will capitalize on your strengths and in which your weaknesses are not major requirements of the job. This type of analysis will help you develop your career objective(s). The career objective is a specific statement of what type of job you are seeking. The career objective serves as the basis for writing both the resume and the application letter.

Writing the Resume

The style and content of resumes may vary widely, but most resumes will contain:

1. Identifying information

The person's name, address, and telephone number generally are placed at the top of the resume.

2. Statement of career objective

The statement specifies the type of position the applicant is seeking.

3. Summary of education

The summary of education generally includes the diploma and degrees earned, schools attended, and dates. Other educational information such as major courses and grade point averages may be added.

4. Summary of qualifications

The summary of qualifications includes skills, special training, and other qualifications that relate to the career objective.

5. Summary of experience

The summary of jobs held should show how they relate to the career objective.

6. Personal data (optional)

If personal information is to the advantage of the applicant, it should be included. If the personal data is to the disadvantage of the applicant, it should not be included in the resume. For example, a person with excellent health may want to point this out to a prospective employer. On the other hand, a person with a history of frequent illnesses may not want to point this out to a prospective employer. Current laws prevent employers from asking personal questions. Laws do not prevent the applicant from volunteering the same information.

7. Information about references

A list of references or a statement on how to obtain a list of references is frequently included in a resume. *References* are persons who know the applicant well and can vouch for the applicant's qualifications, performance record, or character.

The type of resume you write and the way you organize the resume depends on the amount of experience and education you have. Many people use a reverse chronological listing of experience and educational attainment. This type of resume would be excellent for a person who has worked a number of years, and made job changes which reflect a promotion or upward move. For a person who has limited experience or education, the chronological listing emphasizes weaknesses rather than strengths. A resume which emphasizes the job objective and qualifications for the job capitalizes on strengths and minimizes weaknesses.

Compare the resumes on pages 162 and 163.

Comparison

The resume prepared for Dale Best is better for a person with little experience. It places major emphasis on education and qualifications to do the job.

The resume prepared for Judy Helm uses experience to show her sales qualifications. Each year from the time she finished school to the present is accounted for, and each job shows advancement.

Letter of Application

Few, if any, companies will hire a person on the basis of a letter of application. It is doubtful that any company would hire an individual without seeing or talking to the individual. Therefore, the main purpose of the application letter is to get an interview.

A good approach to use in writing an application letter is:

- Establish a point of contact
- State specifically the type of job you are seeking
- Highlight your major qualifications
- Refer to the resume enclosed
- Request an interview

The point of contact is used to let the employer know how you found out about the job opportunity. If you are writing to determine if a job is open, the point of contact can be used to gain attention and explain why you are interested in that particular company.

It is important to state in specific terms what type of job you are seeking. A letter asking for "any job I might be qualified for" makes a poor first impression.

The qualifications section of the letter should highlight your major achievements. Most companies are looking for results oriented employees. You can demonstrate that you are accustomed to achieving good results.

The resume provides more detailed information in an objective style. A simple reference to the resume is all that is needed. The idea of additional information helps to increase the desire of the employer to interview you.

The final step is to request an interview in a confident, positive manner. The letter should give the subtle implication of *"when* do you want to interview me" rather than the uncertain *"if* you want to interview me."

The application letter should be typed on plain paper. It is considered to be in poor taste to use present company letterhead.

The letters on pages 164 and 165 are designed to be cover letters for the two resumes previously illustrated.

It is important to analyze and match your qualifications and the requirements of the job. The individuals given an interview will be the ones who demonstrate they are qualified for the job available. Therefore, model application letters should not be copied. The use of the model helps you to think through the process before writing your application letter.

RESUME

DALE BEST
6084 Karen Drive
Springfield, Illinois 62703-4431
217-787-4632

CAREER OBJECTIVE:

To be a word processing technician in a large, centralized word processing center.

QUALIFICATIONS:

Developed good English skills--knowledge of office procedures and accounting, typewrite accurately at 75 words per minute, can operate four brands of automatic typewriters--Oaks, Kent, Holt, and Shay.

EDUCATION:

Springfield High School, May, 1980. Majored in business education and graduated with a "B" average. Served as President of the Future Business Leaders of America and Business Manager of the yearbook.

EXPERIENCE:

Typist   Mills Equipment Company, May, 1980 to present. Typed general correspondence, invoices, and reports for sales and production departments.

Desk Clerk   Dexter Hotel, summers 1978 and 1979. Answered telephone, welcomed guests, processed check-in and check-out forms.

*PERSONAL:

Birth Date: June 25, 1962   Health: Excellent
Marital Status: Married   Children: None
Hobbies: Swimming, jogging and reading

REFERENCES:

References including former employers and teachers provided upon request.

*Note: The individual chose to offer personal information.
         A company cannot request it.

RESUME

JUDY HELM
8421 Walter Street
Memphis, TN 38108-9079
901-762-2464

CAREER OBJECTIVE:

To become a sales manager. Will consider position as an assistant sales manager with opportunity for promotion.

EDUCATION:

Lambert Technical Institute, certificate May, 1969. Majored in business administration.

Houston Academy, diploma June, 1978. Majored in business education.

EXPERIENCE:

Tennessee Sprinkler Company
    1979-Present   Assistant Sales Manager. Coordinated activities of the Middle Tennessee Sales Team.
    1977-1979   Senior Account Executive. Sold sprinklers to high volume distributors.
    1976-1977   Account Representative. Named Sales Representative of the Year.

Lagletter Electronics, Incorporated
    1974-1976   Senior Sales Representative. Sold calculators to educational institutions.
    1972-1974   Sales Representative. Sold calculators in geographic territory.
    1969-1972   Bookkeeper, Sales Department. Recorded all orders, verified invoices, and handled all sales data for commission records.

REFERENCES: (by permission)

Mr. Clyde McBride   Mr. George Lagletter
Tennessee Sprinkler Company   Lagletter Electronics, Incorporated
1842 Willard Drive   8742 Shepard Drive
Memphis, TN 38118-5154   Austin, TX 78753-6880

Mrs. Beverly Talbert, Business Teacher
Lambert Technical Institute
410 Crawford Street
Richmond, VA 23222-5028

6084 Karen Drive
Springfield, IL 62703-4431
March 20, 19--

Mr. Mark Baldwin, Manager
Data and Word Processing Operations
South-Western Insurance Company
1000 Madison
Springfield, IL 62702-5666

Dear Mr. Baldwin:

During my senior year at Springfield High School, our class took a
field trip to your word processing center. At that time, I became
very interested in word processing and decided to develop the skills
necessary to become a word processing technician. Now that I have
the skills, I would like to be considered for a position as a word
processing technician in your center.

I can typewrite accurately at 75 words per minute and have excellent
communication skills. I enjoy the challenge of working with new,
sophisticated equipment and have experience working on four different brands of automatic typewriters. My resume provides additional
details about my qualifications and experience.

Please let me know when it would be convenient to come in for an
interview.

                              Sincerely,

                              Dale Best

                              Dale Best

LETTER OF APPLICATION

8421 Walter Street
Memphis, TN 38108-9079
April 20, 19--

Mr. Albert Rhone
Rhone Lawn and Garden Tools
410 Greenwood Avenue
Richmond, VA 23222-5382

Dear Mr. Rhone:

Mrs. Beverly Talbert, one of my former business teachers at Lambert
Technical Institute, indicated that you have a position available
in sales management. Rhone Lawn and Garden Tools has an outstanding
reputation for quality lawn and garden tools, and I would like very
much to be a sales manager in such a respected firm.

My experience uniquely qualifies me for the position of sales manager
with your firm. In addition to my training in sales management, I
have successfully sold lawn products as a general sales representative
and as a high volume account executive. As assistant manager, I
coordinated the sales efforts of twelve sales representatives and
account executives. My sales team increased its sales volume by 40
percent in the last two years.

The enclosed resume provides additional information about my qualifications for a position with your company. I plan to move back to
Richmond on Wednesday and would be available for an interview any
day next week. Please let me know what day and time would be most
convenient for you.

                    Sincerely,

                    Judy Helm

                    Ms. Judy Helm

Enclosure

APPLICATION LETTER

Application Blank

Many companies have developed an application form which must be completed by each job applicant. The application blank often duplicates information that is included in the resume. Companies require completed application forms for several reasons:

1. Not all applicants provide a resume.
2. Applicants can select the information they choose to provide in a resume.
3. Uniform information is available on each applicant which facilitates comparison of qualifications.
4. The company is provided with a sample of the applicant's work. Writing skills, organizational ability, neatness, and other characteristics can be judged.

The person who has prepared a resume is in a much better position to complete the application form than the person who has not gone through the self-analysis process required for the resume.

In an effort to avoid discriminatory practices in hiring, most companies have deleted all items on the application blank that ask for personal information. Some companies have replaced these items with a statement from applicants explaining why they are qualified for the job or outlining career goals for the next few years.

The application blank on pages 167 and 168 was completed by Dale Best. Notice how easy it is to complete the blank using the information that is already organized on the resume.

Other Communications Used in the Job Application Process

A number of other types of communications may be written in the job application process. Three frequently written communications are: follow-up letter after the interview, request for information from references, and letter of recommendation. The models presented in Chapters 2 and 3 for writing positive and routine letters can be used for writing these three types of communications.

Follow-up Letter

Many applicants granted an interview write a short thank-you note expressing appreciation for the time given them and confirming interest in the position. The thank-you letter should be short, friendly, and sincere. A letter that is an overstatement of thanks produces a negative effect. The thank-you letter can also be used as an opportunity to provide additional information.

Request for Information

Employers often write letters requesting information from references listed by applicants. The letter may be a cover letter for a form to be completed, or it may simply be an open-ended request for information about the applicant.

Common courtesy requires that applicants request permission before listing an individual as a reference. Therefore, the prospective employer generally can be reasonably sure that the reference listed is willing to provide information about the applicant.

The request for information will generally identify the applicant, describe the position available, and ask for an assessment of the applicant's capabilities, character, or performance record.

Letter of Recommendation

Employers frequently are asked to provide information about former employees. If a form is provided, it is completed and returned. If a form is not provided, a letter is generally written.

The letter of recommendation normally:

1. Identifies the applicant.
2. Explains the professional relationship between the applicant and reference.
3. Indicates how long the applicant has been known.
4. Assesses the capabilities, character, or performance of the applicant.
5. Makes a recommendation to the prospective employer.

The letters on pages 169, 170, and 171 illustrate three communications commonly used in the job application process.

Springfield Insurance Company

Application for Employment

Name: _Dale Best_   **Telephone:** _217-787-4632_

Address: _6084 Karen Drive_   **Social Security Number:** _436-82-7041_

Springfield, Ill. 62703-4431

Position Applying for: _Word processing technician_

Education: (List in reverse chronological order.)

School	Location	Degree	Dates
Springfield High	Springfield, Ill.	Diploma	1976-1980

Work Experience: (Give company, address, dates, position, and major duties for each job held.)

Mills Equipment Company, 302 Monroe Street, E. Springfield, Illinois 62706-4847. Typist. Typed general correspondence, invoices, and reports for sales and production departments, May 1980 to present.

Dexter Hotel, 612 Bonnie Court, Springfield, Illinois 62704-4953. Desk Clerk. Answered the telephone, welcomed guests, processed check-in and check-out forms.

Professional Associations:

Future Business Leaders of America

Yearbook Committee — Journalism Club

Honors, Offices, Special Activities:

Secretary, Vice President, and President of Future

Business Leaders of America

Business Manager — Yearbook

Honor List — "B" Average

Special Training, Skills, Qualifications:

Good English skills; typewrite 75 words per minute

accurately; knowledge of office procedures and

accounting; ability to operate four brands of

automatic typewriters

Applicant's Statement of Why You Should Be Hired:

I believe I should be hired because my knowledge

of word processing, my excellent English and typing

skills, and my desire to be a good word pro-

cessing technician will enable me to be a very

productive employee for your company.

References:

1. Mr. Scott Mills, Mills Equipment Company
   302 Monroe Street, E., Springfield, Illinois 62706-4847
2. Mrs. Anna Levine, General Manager, Dexter Hotel
   612 Bonnie Court, Springfield, Illinois 62704-4953
3. Mr. Amos Tassen, Business Teacher, Springfield High
   School, 123 Circle Drive, Springfield, Illinois 62703-4545

8421 Walter Street
Memphis, TN 38108-9079
May 1, 19--

Mr. Albert Rhone
Rhone Lawn and Garden Tools
410 Greenwood Avenue
Richmond, VA 23222-5382

Dear Mr. Rhone:

I appreciate the courtesies you extended to me. After talking with
you about the position of sales manager, I am even more convinced
that I can make a significant contribution to Rhone Lawn and Garden
Tools.

Yesterday, I received a letter signed by every member of my sales
team at the Tennessee Sprinkler Company. I am enclosing a copy of
the letter because I believe you will be interested in their reaction
to my leadership.

I look forward to hearing from you, and I hope you will give me the
opportunity to demonstrate that I can be an effective sales manager
for Rhone Lawn and Garden Tools.

Sincerely,

Judy Helm

Ms. Judy Helm

Enclosure

FOLLOW-UP LETTER

Rhone
Lawn and Garden Tools

410 Greenwood Avenue
Richmond, Virginia   23222-5382

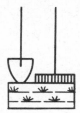

April 28, 19--

Mrs. Beverly Talbert, Business Teacher
Lambert Technical Institute
410 Crawford Street
Richmond, VA 23222-5028

Dear Mrs. Talbert:

When Ms. Judy Helm applied for a position in sales management with
our company, she listed your name as a reference. Would you please
complete the enclosed form giving us your evaluation of Ms. Helm?

I hope to make a decision within two weeks. Hopefully, you can
assist by providing information which will help me to evaluate her
leadership capabilities.

I look forward to hearing from you.

                                    Sincerely,

                                    Albert Rhone

                                    Albert Rhone

ac

Enclosure

REQUEST FOR INFORMATION

**TENNESSEE
SPRINKLER COMPANY**

1842 WILLARD DRIVE • MEMPHIS, TENNESSEE 38118-5154

May 3, 19--

Mr. Albert Rhone
Rhone Lawn and Garden Tools
410 Greenwood Avenue
Richmond, VA 23222-5382

Dear Mr. Rhone:

It is indeed a pleasure for me to give Judy Helm an outstanding
recommendation.

Judy was hired in 1976 and was named Sales Representative of the
Year in her first year with our company. She continued to advance
each year in the company. In addition to her natural talent in
selling, Judy has developed excellent managerial skills. She has
a pleasing personality, a positive attitude, and an excellent work
ethic.

We regret very much that Judy has decided to return to her hometown.
We believe that she would have moved rapidly into a top-management
position in our firm. Should Judy ever decide to return to Memphis,
we would be delighted to hire her again.

                           Sincerely,

                           Clyde McBride

                           Clyde McBride
                           General Manager

dm

LETTER OF RECOMMENDATION

Application:

I. Review of Basic Guides to Better Letters and Memos

In this chapter, Guide 8, "Use Words Efficiently," and Guide 10, "Keep Up with Trends in Writing," are reviewed. You may want to review the material on pages 23 and 30 of Chapter 1 before completing the following exercises.

Use Words Efficiently

Rewrite the following sentences to make them more concise.

1. Please make an announcement to the employees that the managers will take into consideration all employee suggestions before making a decision.

_____

_____

_____

_____

_____

2. In the majority of instances employees can be contacted in a small amount of time due to the fact that we have installed a new internal communications system.

_____

_____

_____

_____

_____

3. The qualified expert will tell the group that if they revert back to the old approach they can expect again problems exactly identical to the ones experienced last year.

_____

_____

_____

_____

_____

4. The report that was eight pages in length dealt with temperature variations in the city of San Juan, Puerto Rico.

_____

_____

_____

_____

_____

5. The report was restricted and limited to a study of the problems and concerns pertaining to the shortage of power and energy.

_____

_____

_____

_____

_____

Keep Abreast of Trends

Review the following sentences using contemporary language and making them sex fair.

6. Pursuant to your request, I have enclosed herewith an analysis of competitive products.

_____

_____

_____

_____

_____

7. A female attorney from the Legal Aid Society represented the customer service girl in the discrimination suit.

_____

_____

_____

_____

_____

8. We trust that you will kindly advise us of any changes.

_____

_____

_____

_____

_____

9. The stewardess served coffee to the salesmen.

_____

_____

_____

_____

_____

10. Attached please find a copy of the report submitted by the male nurse.

_____

_____

_____

_____

_____

II. Complete the following assignments related to the job application process:

1. Analyze your strengths and skills and write a career objective statement.
2. Look through the classified ad section of the newspaper and find an ad for a position that is in line with your career objective. Clip it out.
3. Prepare a resume that you could use in applying for the job you clipped out of the paper. Make it factual.
4. Write a letter of application to send with the resume. If a name is not given in the ad, make up an appropriate name and title.
5. Complete the application blank on page 177. Use your resume to help you organize the information.
6. You had an interview for the job. During the interview, you were taken to lunch at a nice restaurant. Write a follow-up letter confirming your interest in the job.

Performance Evaluation: Chapter Six

I. Revise the following sentences to make them more concise.

1. We are of the belief that you should make your selection of the winner in the near future.

_____

_____

_____

2. Please make an effort to send an invitation to the spouse of each employee.

_____

_____

_____

3. You will receive a check in the amount of $25 on the occasion of your visit to our company.

_____

_____

_____

4. They will have to cooperate together to receive the maximum possible benefits.

_____

_____

_____

5. The designs selected were triangular in shape and red in color.

_____

_____

_____

II. Revise the following sentences to make them sex fair and use contemporary language.

1. Trusting that this report meets your needs and with my best regards, I remain.

_____

_____

_____

2. The materials are being sent to you under separate cover.

_____

_____

_____

3. I will ask my girl to make copies of the proposal and give it to your serviceman.

_____

_____

_____

4. The lady doctor who operated on me is very competent.

_____

_____

_____

5. Businessmen should contact their Congressmen and ask them to support the legislation.

_____

_____

_____

III. Read the following job notices from the classified section of the newspaper.

1.

**WANTED—SECRETARY TO
PLANT MANAGER**

Excellent paying position for ambitious secretary with
good typewriting, shorthand, and English skills. Send
resume and letter of application to: Mrs. Cecilia
Meyers, Personnel Manager, Oxford Industries, 820
Main Street, Your City, State, and Zip Code.

2.

**WANTED—ASSISTANT TO
OFFICE MANAGER**

An excellent training position for a high school
graduate. Courses and/or experience in business desirable. Send your resume and letter of application to Mr.
William Debuck, Office Manager, 208 Main Street,
Your City, State, and Zip Code.

Select one of the positions advertised and apply for it.

IV. You were granted an interview for the position. During the interview you were asked to have two
people send letters of recommendation. Write a letter to one of the individuals you would use as a
reference and ask that individual to send a letter of recommendation to the person listed in the ad.

V. Write a follow-up letter after the interview giving the names and titles of the two individuals who will be
sending letters of recommendation.

Springfield Insurance Company

Application for Employment

Name: _____   Telephone: _____

Address: _____   Social Security Number: _____

_____

Position Applying for: _____

Education: (List in reverse chronological order.)

School	Location	Degree	Dates

Work Experience: (Give company, address, dates, position, and major duties for each job held.)

_____

_____

_____

_____

_____

_____

_____

_____

_____

_____

_____

_____

_____

_____

Professional Associations:

_____

_____

_____

Honors, Offices, Special Activities:

_____

_____

_____

_____

Special Training, Skills, Qualifications:

_____

_____

_____

_____

_____

Applicant's Statement of Why You Should Be Hired:

_____

_____

_____

_____

_____

_____

_____

References:

1. _____

_____

2. _____

_____

3. _____

_____

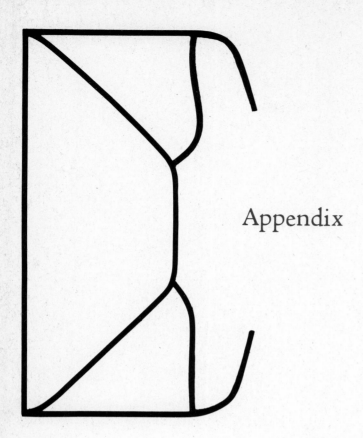

Appendix

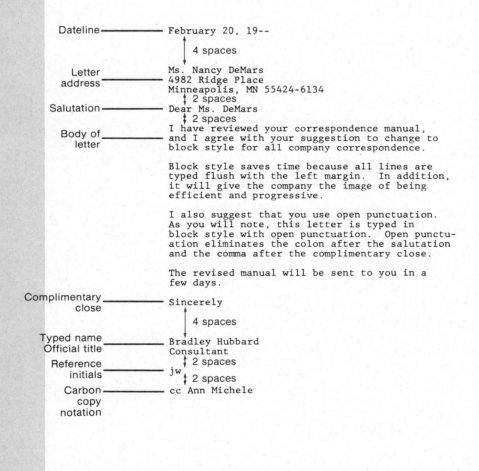

HUBBARD AND ASSOCIATES

2599 MIDWAY ROAD
DULUTH, MN 55810-5957

Dateline ———————— February 20, 19--

↕ 4 spaces

Letter
address ———————— Ms. Nancy DeMars
4982 Ridge Place
Minneapolis, MN 55424-6134
↕ 2 spaces

Salutation ———————— Dear Ms. DeMars
↕ 2 spaces

Body of ——————— I have reviewed your correspondence manual,
letter   and I agree with your suggestion to change to
block style for all company correspondence.

Block style saves time because all lines are
typed flush with the left margin. In addition,
it will give the company the image of being
efficient and progressive.

I also suggest that you use open punctuation.
As you will note, this letter is typed in
block style with open punctuation. Open punctuation eliminates the colon after the salutation
and the comma after the complimentary close.

The revised manual will be sent to you in a
few days.

Complimentary ——————— Sincerely
close

↕ 4 spaces

Typed name ——————— Bradley Hubbard
Official title   Consultant
↕ 2 spaces
Reference ——————— jw
initials   ↕ 2 spaces
Carbon ——————— cc Ann Michele
copy
notation

BLOCK STYLE

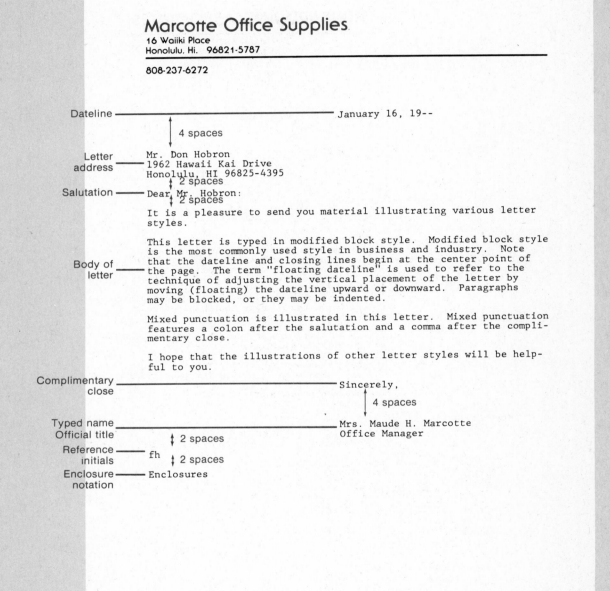

Marcotte Office Supplies
16 Waiiki Place
Honolulu, Hi. 96821-5787

808-237-6272

Dateline ———————————————————— January 16, 19--

↕ 4 spaces

Letter
address ——— Mr. Don Hobron
1962 Hawaii Kai Drive
Honolulu, HI 96825-4395
↕ 2 spaces
Salutation ——— Dear Mr. Hobron:
↕ 2 spaces
It is a pleasure to send you material illustrating various letter
styles.

This letter is typed in modified block style. Modified block style
is the most commonly used style in business and industry. Note
Body of ——— that the dateline and closing lines begin at the center point of
letter   the page. The term "floating dateline" is used to refer to the
technique of adjusting the vertical placement of the letter by
moving (floating) the dateline upward or downward. Paragraphs
may be blocked, or they may be indented.

Mixed punctuation is illustrated in this letter. Mixed punctuation
features a colon after the salutation and a comma after the complimentary close.

I hope that the illustrations of other letter styles will be helpful to you.

Complimentary ———————————————————— Sincerely,
close
↕ 4 spaces

Typed name ———————————————————— Mrs. Maude H. Marcotte
Official title   Office Manager
↕ 2 spaces
Reference ——— fh ↕ 2 spaces
initials
Enclosure ——— Enclosures
notation

MODIFIED BLOCK STYLE

Hulbert & Hulbert
210 Crestwood Drive/Greensboro NC   27408-6565

Begin all
major lines at
left margin. ————————— March 10, 19--

Begin address   ↕ 3 spaces
3 blank line
spaces below ————————— Professional Services, Inc.
date.   610 Perkins Road
                         Fayetteville, NC 27706-1991

Omit salutation. ———————   ↕ 3 spaces

Subject line in all ——————— AMS SIMPLIFIED LETTER STYLE
capital letters
with a triple space   ↕ 3 spaces
above it
and below it.   Please use the AMS Simplified letter style for
                         all mass mailings that you prepare for us in
                         the future.

                         The Simplified letter style eliminates the
                         problem of selecting a proper salutation. In
                         addition, we think this letter style gives us
                         the image of being progressive and efficient.

Omit   We look forward to receiving the mailing for
complimentary   Project 3220 shortly.
close. ——————————   ↕ 4 spaces

Writer's name and ——————— JACK E. HULBERT, PRESIDENT
title in all caps
at least 3 blank   sk
line spaces
below letter body.

**AMS (ADMINISTRATIVE MANAGEMENT SOCIETY)
SIMPLIFIED LETTER STYLE**

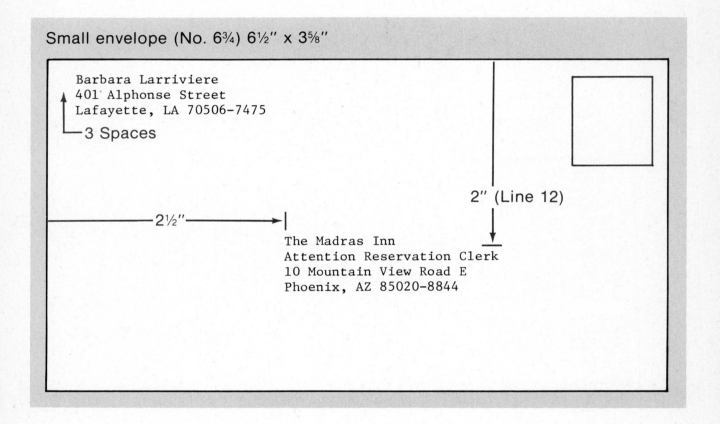

Small envelope (No. 6¾) 6½″ x 3⅝″

Barbara Larriviere
401 Alphonse Street
Lafayette, LA 70506-7475

3 Spaces

2½″

2″ (Line 12)

The Madras Inn
Attention Reservation Clerk
10 Mountain View Road E
Phoenix, AZ 85020-8844

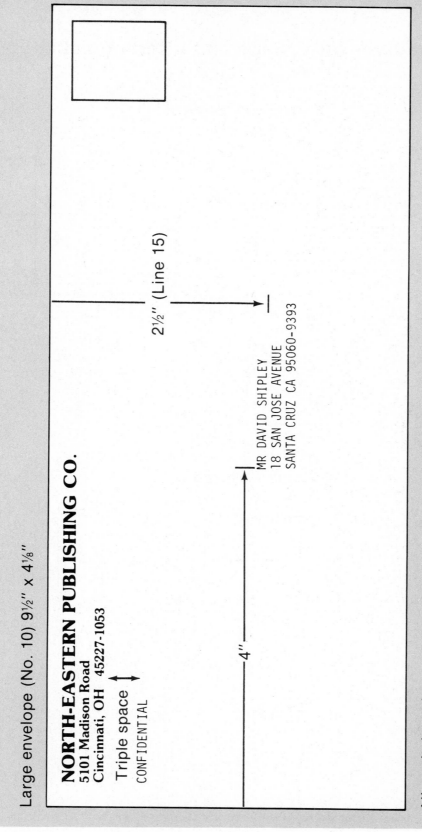

Large envelope (No. 10) 9½″ x 4⅛″

NORTH-EASTERN PUBLISHING CO.
5101 Madison Road
Cincinnati, OH   45227-1053

Triple space
CONFIDENTIAL

4″

2½″ (Line 15)

MR DAVID SHIPLEY
18 SAN JOSE AVENUE
SANTA CRUZ CA 95060-9393

All capitals style recommended by U.S. Postal Service
to aid mechanical mail sorting.

Procedures for Folding and Inserting Letter

Large Envelope

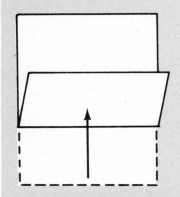

Place letter face up. Fold up from bottom slightly less than 1/3 of sheet.

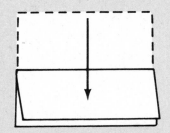

Fold down top to approximately ½ inch of bottom fold.

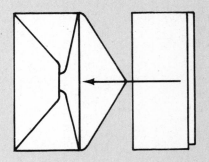

Insert folded edge toward bottom of envelope.

Small Envelope

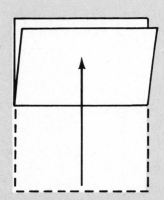

Place letter face down. Fold bottom up to ½ inch from top.

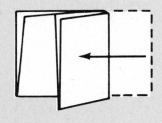

Fold right third to left.

Fold left third to ½ inch from last crease.

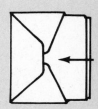

Insert last creased edge first.

Jamestowne Advertising

TO: All Employees

FROM: Jeff Hare

DATE: September 6, 19--

SUBJECT: Interoffice Memo Forms

New interoffice memo forms have been printed and will be distributed this week. Each office will receive two boxes of the forms. Additional forms will be available in the supply room.

The form illustrated in this communication is to be used for communications to all employees located in our main office on Pine Street.

We now have employees located in six branch offices. Please use the form which has our address and telephone number printed at the top for communications to employees in the six branches. The printed address makes it easier for employees in other locations to reply to our messages.

fh

RESUME

MARLENE THOMPSON
6260 North Park Drive
Pennsauken, NJ 08109-8527
609-662-7027

CAREER OBJECTIVE:

To be an executive secretary. Will consider position as a secretary with opportunity to become an executive secretary.

QUALIFICATIONS:

Excellent secretarial and English skills. Typewrite accurately at 70 wpm. Take shorthand at 120 wpm. Knowledge of office procedures and office management.

EDUCATION:

College: Certificate, Middleburg Community College, June, 1979. Majored in business education with a "B" average.

High School: Northeast High School, June, 1978. Majored in business education with a "B" average.

EXPERIENCE:

Steno II Northwood Manufacturers, June, 1979 to present. Perform general secretarial duties. Handle heavy volume of shorthand and typewriting work.

REFERENCES:

References including current employer and former teachers provided upon request.